Secret Passion to

CW01673485

Alan

With all best wishes

and love

Suzanne & Richard

9th August 2002

Ann Sumner & Richard Walker

Secret Passion to Noble Fashion:

The World of the Portrait Miniature

HOLBURNE
MUSEUM OF ART

Holburne Museum of Art, Bath

Phillips
INTERNATIONAL
AUCTIONEERS & VALUERS

Published by
Holburne Museum of Art
Great Pulteney Street
Bath
BA2 4DB

First published 1999

Designed by Richard Chlupaty, Bournemouth
Printed by BAS Printers Limited, Over Wallop, Stockbridge, Hants
Set in Monotype Garamond

Ann Sumner and Richard Walker
Secret Passion to Noble Fashion: The World of the Portrait Miniature
1. Art - Europe - 17th to 19th century
ISBN: 0 9517574 31

Cover illustrations: Andrew Plimer, *Lady in White Wearing a Miniature* and its reverse (catalogue no. 60)

Contents

Acknowledgements
Ann Sumner
7

A Note from the Collector
9

The Changing Role of the Portrait Miniature
Ann Sumner
11

A Private Collection of Miniatures
Richard Walker
37

Contents of the Catalogue
43

The Catalogue
Richard Walker
45

Bibliography
228

Index of Artists
229

Index of Portraits
230

Acknowledgements

The present exhibition affords the opportunity to present to the public for the first time just over a hundred superb portrait miniatures from a private collection. It has been a privilege for me to have had the opportunity to view these miniatures regularly over recent years and to see the collection expand and develop, thus sharing in the excitement of new purchases. It is now an even greater pleasure to see this collection so finely displayed at the Holburne Museum for the enjoyment of a wider audience. We are deeply indebted to the Private Collector for selecting this museum as the Bath venue for this exhibition and allowing us to complement the display with miniatures from the Holburne's own rare collection. In addition the Collector has also generously contributed to the administration and display costs. We are also very grateful to Phillips International Fine Art Auctioneers for their sponsorship. They have played a key role in supporting this exhibition from its conception and their active encouragement is much appreciated.

I have been fascinated by miniatures since curating the exhibition *Death, Passion and Politics* at the Dulwich Picture Gallery in 1995. This exhibition drew my attention to the wearing of portrait miniatures as part of the mourning process, and it considered in particular how Sir Kenelm Digby used miniatures after the death of his wife. Since then I have been interested in the social usage and display of miniatures in the seventeenth and eighteenth centuries. I am greatly indebted to those scholars who have written on the subject, most especially Katherine Coombs, Ian Dejardin, Sebastian Edwards, Stephen Lloyd, John Murdoch and Aileen Ribeiro. I have been particularly encouraged to pursue my research by Emma Rutherford, miniatures expert at Phillips International, whose advice throughout has been much appreciated; by Richard Walker with whom it has been a very great pleasure to work on this exhibition; and by the Private Collector himself. Both Richard Walker and I owe a great debt of gratitude to three colleagues of ours at the National Portrait Gallery, Jacob Simon, Jill Springnall and Tim Moreton, who have given of their time and expertise and whose help has been invaluable. It has also been a pleasure for me to work with the designer of this exhibition, George Carter, who has so sensitively and imaginatively displayed these miniatures, and with Montague Shaw, Richard Chlupaty and Patricia Verity on the production of this exhibition catalogue.

I would like also to thank the many others who have worked for a long period of time on the exhibition and with the production of the catalogue: namely Rachel Boom, David Dawson, Patricia Eaton, Julia Findlater, Kate Harris, Kathleen Kuys, Alastair Laing, Emma Lauze, David Lavender, Michael Letendrie, Trevor Reynolds, Susan Santini, Ann Smith, Celia Stern, Helen White, Nicholas White, Hayden Williams; also Colin Wilson and Nick Nicholson at the University of Bath Photographic Department. My greatest thanks are extended to my patient and hard-working colleagues at the museum who have done so much to help and support me: in particular Philippa Bishop, Joyce Peachey, Jose Angelo-Sparling, Wilf Bates and Sid Rendell. I would also like to thank Jerzy Jan Kierkuc-Bielinski, a student volunteer from the Courtauld Institute, who has devoted many hours in order to help with my research, painstakingly tracking down every image of a miniature he was sent to find. The museum Director, Barley Roscoe, has been a source of strength and encouragement throughout the months of preparation for this exhibition. Most of all I must thank Julia Naismith for her utter commitment and hard work with administration and publicity. It has been a privilege for me to be so involved in this project and my sincere thanks are extended to the Private Collector for giving me this inspiring opportunity to reveal this rare and lovely collection to the public.

Ann Sumner
Keeper of Art
Holburne Museum of Art, Bath
April 1999

A Note from the Collector

I liken collecting to an obsessive disease. One day in the future I am sure medical science will discover a gene with 'Collector' stamped all over it! Ever since I can remember I have collected something. It started at school with cigarette cards, graduated to penknives and then on to antique daggers.

My interest in art began in 1964 when I was eighteen years old and fresh out of boarding school. It was aimed almost exclusively at portraiture. Miniatures fascinated me: they display such sensitivity and beauty. In those days they were inexpensive to buy and I soon built up a line of credit with various dealers, which was the only way I could afford to collect. Over the years the collection grew and so did my knowledge, although even now when I speak to experts like Richard Walker and David Lavender I realise how little I know and how much there is to learn.

In 1979 what I had always feared occurred. My house was burgled and my collection stolen. I was devastated – hence my present status as an anonymous collector. As luck would have it, several months later I was playing tennis at my club with another member, David Lavender, and after the match I asked him what he did for a living. Imagine my surprise when he told me that he specialised in miniatures! That was seventeen years ago, and since then he has advised me, given me the opportunity to acquire rare and important works, and guided me in auction purchases. I can honestly say that, even now, I very rarely buy anything without first consulting him. I welcome this opportunity for expressing my gratitude to him.

In 1996 I went with David and our wives to a Charity recital at Wells Cathedral. On the way David insisted that we visit the Holburne Museum in Bath. I was very impressed by the palatial eighteenth-century building housing a collection which so effectively complements its period. It was a pleasure to meet Dr Ann Sumner, the Keeper of Art, who is almost as obsessed by the subject of miniatures as I am. Her drive, industry and enthusiasm have enabled this exhibition to take place. It was Ann who was instrumental in persuading Richard Walker, a legend in the world of miniatures, to catalogue my collection. It was a privilege to meet and work with him. I stand humbled by his mastery of the subject obtained through decades of experience and research. Thank you, Richard.

Space is always a problem for a collector, so it is very exciting to see the whole collection displayed together in one room, in an exhibition imaginatively designed by George Carter. I would like to express my thanks to him and to all those at the Holburne Museum who have worked so hard to make this exhibition possible, especially to Barley Roscoe, the Museum's Director, and to Julia Naismith, who has been responsible for publicity and administration.

Finally, a word about the auction house, Phillips International. As a young collector with very little money I was often treated rather dismissively by some dealers and large auction houses. Phillips, however, always had time for the small collector and have continued to be generous with their expertise. Some of my finest miniatures came from their auction rooms. Quite correctly they take the view that by encouraging young collectors, as in my case, these collectors will retain a wealth of goodwill and continue to turn to that company for support in expanding their collections. My thanks to Phillips for their generous sponsorship of this exhibition and to their miniatures expert Emma Rutherford for her guidance.

I very much hope that visitors to the exhibition will experience some of the excitement and pleasure that I have derived over the years whilst assembling this collection of miniatures.

April 1999

The Changing Role of the Portrait Miniature

Ann Sumner

Introduction

The present exhibition of superb portrait miniatures dating from the early seventeenth through to the nineteenth century has been beautifully displayed thanks to the skill of the exhibition designer, George Carter. While conscious of the high level of security required for the cases, he has also perfected the lighting for the modern exhibition visitor and each individual miniature is shown to full advantage with its perfect brushwork and subtle colours. Examining miniatures today in such an exhibition setting, carefully admiring the techniques used to create them, is to be looking at them very much out of their historical context, for the role of the portrait miniature has changed fundamentally over the centuries. It is quite different from observing a full-scale seventeenth- or eighteenth-century portrait. Although both may faithfully illustrate the features of a beautiful young man or woman, dressed in the height of fashion, the full-scale portrait was always intended to be hung on the wall for public viewing while the smaller and more intimate version was often conceived for private contemplation. Perhaps the nearest equivalent to the miniature today is the valued wallet photograph, sometimes worn and crumpled, but lovingly displayed within the intimacy of a personal everyday item.

The Fashion Accessory – Miniatures set in Jewels and Boxes

Early in the sixteenth century portrait miniatures were placed in small turned ivory boxes for their protection. Such miniatures remained thus stored well into the seventeenth century, as Laurence Hilliard's Will of 1647 records. Amongst the items he bequeathed were 'my own picture drawn when I was a young man in an ivory box' and one of 'my grandfather Hilliard in an ivory box with a crystal upon it'. Such boxes could be carried in a pouch or worn about a woman's waist, for the beauty of a miniature was that, compared to a full-scale painting, it was portable and intimate enough to be carried upon one's own person. Other miniatures were set into picture boxes or ornate jewels and worn as part of the rich Elizabethan costume. In contemporary portraiture most jewel boxes are worn closed in a secretive manner; but it was in fact no secret at all as to whose image was usually inside. Towards the end of Elizabeth I's reign the wearing of her miniature was *de rigueur*. In a portrait miniature of *Francis Drake* (1586–7) on loan to the Victoria and Albert Museum, the sitter wears a carved onyx jewel containing a miniature of Elizabeth I which was not visible unless the jewel, which bears the head of a negro, was opened. Others, such as the *Armada Jewel,* survive in the Victoria and Albert Museum (V & A M81–1935). Such personal loyalty tokens to the monarch were part of the court propaganda machine, and the tradition carried on into the Stuart period. Occasionally some survive of a more personal and romantic nature, such as the famous *Gresley Jewel* of 1580–5 (at Southside House) containing a portrait of Sir Thomas Gresley and his bride, Catherine Walsingham, by Nicholas Hilliard. Here both images are secreted within the jewel. This sort of locket containing a miniature was in contemporary accounts usually merely referred to as a 'jewel'; thus when one was presented as a gift it was not always certain whether such a miniature lay within.

In Shakespeare's *Twelfth Night,* written at the very turn of the sixteenth century, Viola dressed in male garb presents a jewel to Olivia saying:

> *Here wear this jewel for me, 'tis my picture,*

by way of explanation. Shakespeare also includes the wearing of miniatures in a famous scene from *Hamlet*, although in this case the images can clearly be seen. In Act 3, Scene IV, Hamlet confronts his mother Gertrude and tries to show her the difference between her former husband, Hamlet's father, and her present husband, Claudius. In most stage versions he snatches the miniature of Claudius which she is wearing and compares it with his own miniature which he wears of his father:

> *Look here upon this picture and on this –*
> *The counterfeit presentment of two brothers ...*

The contrast is between the perfection of beauty and virtue represented by Hamlet's father and the features of the villainous Claudius:

> *Here is your husband, like a mildew'd ear*
> *Blasting his wholesome brother.*

Katherine Coombs has recently drawn attention to the ancient and much repeated story about Elizabeth I demanding to know the identity of the portrait concealed within one of her ladies' 'jewels'. Queen Elizabeth pinned it to her shoe, thus favouring the young male courtier discovered within the jewel. According to legend the young man wrote a poem dedicated to the Virgin Queen, who showed her thanks by elevating him from her shoe buckle to her elbow, and so closer to her heart.

On the death of the Old Queen the miniature as an art form, courtly propaganda

[1]
Portrait of Thomas Lyte
Unknown Artist, 1611
Somerset County Museum Service

token and fashionable jewel did not decline, although the quality of the royal miniature did so to some extent. *The Ark Locket* of *c.* 1605–10 from the studio of Nicholas Hilliard in the Victoria and Albert Museum (V & A M92–1975) is hardly comparable with some of the great Elizabethan jewels. There is, however, the famous *Lyte Jewel* made of gold, enamel and diamonds which contains a portrait of high quality of James I by Hilliard, now in the British Museum. It can also be seen being worn by its owner, the historian Thomas Lyte of Lytes Cary in Somerset. This portrait, by an unknown artist, usually hangs in the Great Hall of the Castle Museum in Taunton (illustration 1). The jewel was presented to the sitter on 12 July 1610 as a reward for the historian's gift to the King of a manuscript tracing the dynastic roots of the house of Stuart. A contemporary, Philip Gawdy, recorded one similar occasion on which

> *some knights and other gentlemen of the King's servants, to number of sixteen, had chains given them by the King with his picture hanging by to the value of thirty or forty pound. All the rest had his picture only.*

This portrait, on loan to this exhibition from Somerset County Museums Service, was commissioned in honour of that occasion and is dated April 14th, 1611. It is one of the last examples of a male courtier proudly painted with his sovereign's 'jewel'. The pendant is a tri-lobed drop set with diamonds. From this time onwards the wearing of a miniature in a 'picture box' became very much the domain of women who incorporated it as a fashion accessory, and it was particularly popularised by James I's wife, Queen Anne of Denmark.

Anne was a woman of considerable character and artistic taste who established her own Court quite distinct from that of King James and appointed Peter Oliver as 'Queen's painter for the art of limning' in 1605. Portrayed by Isaac Oliver right at the beginning of her husband's reign, she openly indicates a small locket around her neck which is presumed to contain an image. Tied in a bow on her bosom is another larger jewel which anticipates those she wears in portraits 'in large' (National Portrait Gallery, 4010). She also encouraged the presentation of miniatures of herself by Hilliard set in Elizabethan-type 'jewels'. One such which has survived is one of the most accomplished miniatures by the elderly Hilliard (now in the Fitzwilliam Museum, No. 3855). The jewelled case is set with table diamonds and bears the monograms of Anne, her mother Sophia and her brother Christian of Denmark. Anne appears to have presented it to one of her ladies-in-waiting, Lady Anne Livingston, Countess of Eglinton. The Queen presented it later as a wedding present in 1612 and Lady Anne, in a full-scale portrait, wears the miniature case tied to a ribbon knotted in a bow with a pendant pear pearl above her heart.

In picture after picture, Queen Anne can be seen wearing the familiar large miniature case which so much more obviously contains the image of a loved one than the elaborate Elizabethan 'jewels'. Anne appears to have begun this trend at the time of the premature death of her son Henry, Prince of Wales, and is shown in mourning with such a miniature case in Marcus Gheeraerts' painting of 1612–13 (National Portrait Gallery, 4656). A more elaborate miniature case with a pearl drop attached occurs in Gheeraets' full-length portrait of her at Woburn Abbey, *c.*1614. The same early mourning miniature recurs in the famous portrait of her after Paul van Somer of 1617 (National Portrait Gallery, 127, illustration 2). Again, it is tied to her bodice with a small bow and presumably contains the image of her much-mourned son. The painting is renowned for the depiction of her jewellery, including many famous pieces such as the Christian IV monogram brooch which also occurs in the Woburn picture. On the Queen's own death in 1619 one of her ladies-in-waiting, Elizabeth Grey, Countess of Kent, wears a miniature box decorated with Anne's emblem in a portrait of her by Paul van Somer (Tate Gallery, Too 398).

The wearing of such larger portrait miniature boxes prominently on the bosom, near the heart, became a popular show of mourning even after full mourning dress had been abandoned. Some sitters were renowned for such boxes. Elizabeth Vernon, Countess of Southampton (1572–1655), one of the great beauties of the court of Elizabeth I, wears one in the portrait at Sherborne Castle, and again in Gheeraerts' portrait of her (1618) in a feigned oval now at Woburn Abbey. This miniature case is rather plain, as is the one which can be seen in the portrait of *Lettice, Lady Offaly*, another famous widow whose portrait is displayed at the Digby family seat at Sherborne in Dorset. As an elderly and perhaps old-fashioned woman, she is portrayed wearing such a miniature case still in the late 1640s long after they went out of fashion. A much more elaborate case can be seen in a portrait by the successful Scottish miniaturist George Jameson of *Anne Erskine, Countess of Rothes, with her two children, Margaret and John* of 1626 in the Scottish National Portrait Gallery (illustration 3). Thus, even she, in the mid-1620s, was perhaps a little old-fashioned in her highly decorative attire. What is particularly interesting about this painting is not the portrait miniature case she wears as part of her costume, but the miniatures so clearly displayed upon the wall behind her. Here a set of portrait miniatures surround an allegorical subject, also painted in miniature. The lady and her children are clearly shown in a 'cabinet' room where other precious items are stored in the open casket on the table.

By the late 1620s to early 1630s changes in fashion produced a much more restrained elegant attire for men and women in costume and jewellery. This meant that the wearing of the kind of miniature that Lady Erskine displays became outmoded. Miniatures were to lose their secretive appeal and would no longer be concealed but worn as fashion accessories or, more often, as mourning tokens. They were also to find a more permanent, protected home in the setting of the connoisseur's cabinet in rooms very much like the one in which Lady Erskine stands. Such miniatures as these framed upon the wall were clearly never intended to be worn, as their ebony frames indicate. Jameson also portrayed himself, in a self-portrait in the Earl of Seafield's collection, pointing to framed miniatures and a small allegorical work upon the wall indicating that the room is a cabinet.

With the exception of Charles I's cabinet, the most famous connoisseur's closet of the 1630s was that designed at Ham House by the courtier Will Murray, which contained among other treasures a dazzling miniature by Hilliard of *Elizabeth I*. Murray was a particular favourite of Charles I, who had come to the throne in 1624 and had, by the mid-1630s, established a cabinet at Whitehall with seventy-five miniatures as well as bronzes, coins, books, engraved gems and ivories. While the majority of the miniatures were portraits, some were not. Peter Oliver had been expressly commissioned to paint larger 'cabinet'-sized miniatures after paintings by Titian, Caravaggio and Raphael, which were kept alongside Isaac Oliver's superb portraits of the royal family. This magnificent 'museum' of the miniature from Holbein to the superb miniatures by John Hoskins of Charles I and his wife, Queen Henrietta Maria, was dispersed at the end of the Civil War.

The Miniature as a Mourning Token

While the miniature retreated in some respects into the connoisseur's private domain, it remained in the 1620s and 1630s as a powerful and clearly visible mourning device. Several high-profile deaths took place during the period which were openly marked by a miniature no longer concealed in a jewel or box. On 16 February 1624, on the very day that Parliament was due to open, one of the most prominent statesmen at the Court of James I, Ludovic Stuart, Duke of Richmond and Lennox, died unexpectedly in his bed. He was fifty years old. As a mark of respect the opening of Parliament was delayed and his wife, Frances Howard, went into deep and prolonged mourning. In the famous full-length portrait of her in the style of Van Dyck at Longleat she is shown in widow's attire, the only relief to her black costume being the strings of pearls and white ruff and cuffs (illustration 4). Pinned very prominently over her chest is a heart-shaped miniature by Isaac Oliver (now in the National Portrait Gallery, 3663). Two head-and-shoulders versions after the Longleat painting exist, one passing through the London sale rooms in 1972 and the other at Ranger's House, Blackheath (English Heritage). In the latter picture the miniature has actually been cut out of the canvas. A further full-length portrait of the Duchess by Cornelius Johnson, still in mourning but in lighter costume as black was not

[2]
Queen Anne of Denmark
Unknown Artist, 1617
By Courtesy of the National Portrait Gallery, London

[3]
Lady Anne Erskine, Countess of Rothes and her Children
George Jameson, 1626
Scottish National Portrait Gallery, Edinburgh

obligatory for mourning, and wearing the same heart-shaped miniature of her dear departed husband, tied with ribbon to her bodice, is today in the city of Tulsa Art Gallery, Oklahoma, U.S.A. The Duchess died in 1638 and was buried in the same grave as her husband. This very public mourning and the commissioning of numerous portraits, showing her wearing the same miniature, marked a watershed in noble mourning. The miniature was thenceforth prominently revealed as a mourning accessory in its own right with no need for a concealing box.

If Richmond's death was high-profile, it was nothing compared to the general celebrations at the news of the murder in 1628 of the unpopular Duke of Buckingham, Charles I's great favourite. The King mourned deeply, as did the Duchess, but the public lit bonfires to celebrate his stabbing by a disgruntled sailor named Fenton from the abortive La Rochelle expedition. The best-known head and shoulders portrait of the Duchess, in black with a large collar, shows her wearing a prominent portrait of the Duke, not over her heart as the Duchess of Richmond and Lennox had done, but displayed on a large black ribbon in the centre of her stomacher. The painting is by Van Dyck and is owned by the Duke of Rutland. Another threequarter-length version of her, wearing the same miniature, passed through Sotheby's sale rooms in 1935. The most important painting, however, is the group portrait by Van Dyck showing the Duchess and her two sons and one daughter (Rubenshuis, Antwerp). Her children were all later brought up at court with the royal family. A painting of the Duke is displayed on the wall and the Duchess still wears his miniature at the centre of her chest, but here she draws attention to it very deliberately with the thumb and forefinger of her right hand. It is the ultimate symbol of a family bereft of its principal member and the mourning miniature is the main focus of the entire picture.

Prominent women were not the only members of society to mourn deeply and long. Perhaps the most renowned case of prolonged mourning involving miniatures is that of Sir Kenelm Digby. On finding his beautiful wife dead in her bed on Wednesday, 1 May 1633, he immediately commissioned Van Dyck to paint her on her deathbed (Dulwich Picture Gallery 194). At the age of thirty-three the beautiful Venetia had died unexpectedly, causing the rumour that Sir Kenelm had accidentally poisoned her with a viper wine intended to perserve her beauty. In fact she had suffered a cerebral haemorrhage. At night Sir Kenelm slept with this portrait of his wife beside him, lit by candles. In 1635, when he decided to leave England and retreat in deepest mourning to France, he commissioned Peter Oliver to copy the deathbed scene. This miniature is now at Sherborne Castle in Dorset, and Oliver's group portrait miniature of the Digbys with their children, also after Van Dyck, is now in Stockholm. Digby had individual portraits of himself and his wife, after Van

[4]
Frances Howard, Duchess of Lennox and Richmond
Studio of Sir Anthony Van Dyck, circa 1624
By courtesy of the Marquess of Bath, Longleat

[5]
The Exhibition of the Royal Academy at Somerset House
P.A. Martini after John Henry Rambert, 1787
*(Detail over Fireplace)
Royal Academy of Arts, London

Dyck, set in a fine contemporary gold and enamel case. These portable miniatures could then be taken abroad and he could leave the paintings 'in large' behind. They remained his only comfort in his time of despair and darkness. Mourning his wife in this way meant that he almost excluded his sons from his life altogether. He executed a magnificent tomb for Venetia and commissioned a fine family pedigree, but it is the miniatures, produced in her memory after Van Dyck's paintings, which are unique; and it is equally unusual that they have survived in contemporary frames. Horace Walpole recorded his excitement soon after discovering these Digby miniatures in the eighteenth century. He writes that a 'valuable treasure' of miniatures by Isaac and Peter Oliver was 'discovered in an old house in Wales that belonged to one of Kenelm's descendants'. The miniatures,

> *being inclosed in ivory and ebony case, and the whole collection locked up in a wainscot box, they are as perfectly preserved as if newly painted.*

The portrait of *Venetia on her Deathbed* by Peter Oliver after Van Dyck and the double portrait of both Kenelm and Venetia, set in a contemporary frame, now at Sherborne, were both purchased at the Strawberry Hill sale of 1842. When Sir Kenelm died thirty-two years after his wife, having spent twenty of those years in deep mourning, he too was buried in the magnificent tomb he had erected for Venetia in Christchurch, Newgate Street. Sadly this was destroyed in the Great Fire of London.

The Miniature during the Political Upheavals of the Civil War and at the Restoration

While the miniature played an obvious role in the mourning process, it declined in popularity as a fashion accessory and remained very much to be admired in the rarefied climate of the connoisseur's cabinet or in the domain of private contemplation. One is tempted to speculate that Hoskins' miniatures must have been indispensable to the royal couple, Charles I and Henrietta Maria, who spent so much of the Civil War apart, their only contact being by letter. Miniatures of Charles I were mounted and worn during the Civil War. Occasional examples survive, such as a singular one set in a filigree frame from a private collection which was on loan to David Lavender's exhibition in 1993, *The Monarchy in Portrait Miniature.* The wearing of such miniatures would, of course, have been a matter of great delicacy during the tumultuous period of the Civil War.

The accomplished miniaturist David des Granges left London in 1651 after the defeat of the Royalist cause and travelled with Charles II as his unofficial limner. Charles commissioned a number of portrait miniatures of himself to be painted and

[6]
Self Portrait Holding a Miniature
Bernard Lens
The Ashmolean Museum, Oxford

[7]
Queen Charlotte
attributed to Johann Zoffany, circa 1763
Holburne Museum, Bath

circulated among his supporters. By this time Royalists would have been well advised to secrete such miniatures in their cabinets during the Cromwellian rule. Meanwhile in London the greatest miniaturist of the age, Samuel Cooper, was finding favour with Oliver Cromwell, the Lord Protector. Cromwell used Cooper to produce his image, just as Elizabeth I and James I had used Hilliard and Charles I had used Hoskins. A good likeness in miniature was an excellent propaganda tool, and Cooper's miniatures were circulated to supporters and presented as diplomatic gifts. Cooper's response to the very different royal court that was established by Charles II at the Restoration was a much richer style of portraiture. Charles II appointed Cooper as 'King's Limner' and immediately recognised the value of Cooper's miniatures in the presentation of his court style which was so different from the austerity of Cromwell's regime. Cooper was also responsible for the increased size of miniatures during this period, thus making it even less likely that they would return as a fashion accessory. Instead they emerged as significant works of art in their own right, their popularity grew and an amateur interest in them emerged. Ladies even started to have lessons in the art, most notably Mrs Samuel Pepys, who had herself sat to Samuel Cooper and was instructed in the art of miniature painting by Alexander Browne. By the mid eighteenth century it was quite the thing for young ladies to paint fans and their family likenesses in miniature. This genteel pastime became a lifeline for poor female relatives and enabled them to support themselves financially through portrait miniature painting. Upon marriage, however, they were usually encouraged to give up this professional occupation. Some well-known female miniaturists include Diana Dietz, Charlotte Jones and Mrs Mee. Examples of the work by the latter two artists are displayed in the Holburne Museum's miniatures collection.

The Return of the Miniature to Public Display

One of the earliest examples of a female sitter wearing a miniature on her arm is Bernard Lens' *Portrait of Sarah Churchill, Duchess of Marlborough*, dated 1720 (V & A 627–1882). This, however, is clearly a copy after an earlier large oil painting, for by the 1720s the Duchess herself would have been in her sixties and her fashionable attire outdated. On her arm she wears a very large and somewhat cumbersome oval miniature of the Duke, half-way up her forearm rather like a modern bangle. The image was presumably painted at the close of the seventeenth century. During the last years of that century the vulnerability of watercolours on vellum was being noted, especially their susceptibility to damage from light and damp. This fragile form of miniature painting was therefore challenged by two imported techniques from the continent. Initially Charles Boit, who worked for William III, introduced enamel miniatures which were much more durable and with their jewel-like appear-

[8]
Queen Charlotte
Johann Zoffany, 1771
The Royal Collection: Her Majesty The Queen

[9]
Unknown Lady
William Armfield Hobday, Miniature, 1797
The Iveagh Bequest, Kenwood
English Heritage

ance particularly suitable as settings for jewellery, especially bracelets. They also found a perfect home set in the lids of snuff boxes: two examples of miniatures which must have once adorned snuff boxes appear in the current exhibition (catalogue nos. 17 and 18). A little later Bernard Lens introduced the painting on ivory and miniatures diminished in size again until the art form was perfected by such artists as Jeremiah Meyer and Nathaniel Hone. Lens even taught Princess Mary, the daughter of George II, to paint miniatures on ivory. A charming if somewhat naive example of her work, a portrait of her sister, was presented to her mother, set in the lid of a snuff box, an item which survives in the Royal Collection.

Collectors and Miniatures

Despite this new-found development for miniatures, many remained in the protected atmosphere of the cabinet and some evidence is available as to how they were displayed. In a *Self Portrait with his Wife* by the eminent printmaker and antiquarian George Vertue (British Museum), miniatures can be seen hanging on the wall behind the pair. They are displayed in a uniform pattern with three regular rectangular miniatures above one oval miniature in separate segments of the wall space interspersed with Vertue's own prints of noble faces. Other miniature collections are well known and documented, such as that belonging to Horace Walpole. He actually had a special cabinet designed by William Kent in 1743 for the housing of his most prized examples, which he described as a 'new cabinet for my enamels and miniatures'. It is now in the collection of the Victoria and Albert Museum. Other notable collectors of miniatures were Edward Harley, Peter Cross and the Prince of Wales, who in 1743 especially designed a space in his drawing room at Leicester House for the display of miniatures.

By the end of the eighteenth century connoisseurs could go to the Royal Academy to view miniatures openly on display, as is illustrated in Ramberg's well-known image of the public viewing at the Royal Academy show of 1787. A section was particularly reserved for miniatures, all hung tightly together and arranged around the fireplace in the Great Room with large oils surrounding them (illustration 5).

Men and the Portrayal of Miniatures

The entire question of men and miniatures is an interesting one. Although men collected them and were themselves frequently portrayed by miniaturists, they did not wear them openly and were rarely portrayed with them. In the rest of Europe men wore miniatures on a chain about their neck or fastened with a ribbon bow on their breast, whereas men in England generally carried miniatures at the waist together with seals and watches. Sometimes a false watch contained the miniature of a loved one. An example of this is George Engleheart's double portrait of sisters contained within a case that resembles a watch (catalogue nos. 47 and 48). Artists were somewhat the exception to this rule. In the seventeenth century George Jameson had twice portrayed himself with miniatures, once depicting himself in a cabinet where they hung on the wall, and on a second occasion showing himself actually holding a miniature (Aberdeen Museum and Art Gallery). In 1741 George Vertue paints himself in one sketch surrounded by prints and drawings (V & A E2229–1889). He very prominently holds one particular miniature, with an elaborate frame, of his great patron Edward Harley, Earl of Oxford. Some years earlier, in 1720, Bernard Lens had painted himself in a similar manner with the miniature of a female prominently held in his hand (illustration 6). The image is certainly not of his first wife, whose portrait is known, and it is not possible to tell if it is his second wife as no likeness of her is known. However, it has been suggested that it may represent a prominent patron, or someone to whom he gave lessons in the art of miniature painting. Another miniature can be seen below his hand on a table with a brush lying by. The artist may have just completed the miniature and may be holding it up to be admired.

Female Commemoration : The Miniature as Celebratory Fashionable Accessory

The miniature returned to the female wardrobe, not merely as a mourning token, but as a memento of special occasions. The famous portrait of *Mary Panton, Duchess of Ancaster* by Thomas Hudson of 1757, painted to celebrate her attendance at a costume ball at Ranelagh, shows her wearing a miniature of the 2nd Duke, hanging from the waist as part of a chatelaine (Grimsthorpe and Drummond Castle Trust). Perhaps the most famous wearer of miniatures in the mid eighteenth century was Queen Charlotte. At her wedding she wore on the little finger of her right hand a ring with a miniature of George III by Jeremiah Meyer set within it. The King presented his new bride with another miniature of himself, this time set in the round with brilliant cut diamonds, the hardest precious stone equated with fidelity and loyalty, and thus entirely appropriate as a wedding gift. The whole was set in a bracelet of pearls. This miniature is clearly visible being worn on the wrist of the young Queen in the portrait of 1763, attributed to Zoffany, in the Holburne Museum (illustration 7). The queen appears to have another miniature on her other arm as part of a bracelet covered by a glove. In the portrait of her painted many years later in 1771 by Zoffany (Royal Collection 1196, illustration 8), the same miniature is seen again on her right wrist, and recurs in Lawrence's late portrait of 1790 in the National Gallery (4257). It was clearly a most treasured gift throughout her life. In wearing such a miniature bracelet Queen Charlotte adopted a popular form of demonstrating allegiance to another. This is reflected in numerous portraits of sitters wearing miniatures, such as the *Unknown Woman* by Thomas Gainsborough in the Holburne Collection (A66) on display in the exhibition.

The fine settings and concave shapes of two particular miniatures in the current exhibition illustrate how they would have been set as part of gold bracelets (catalogue nos. 36 and 56). Miniatures were also worn as brooches, or more commonly as pendants to a necklace. An idea of how fine the settings could be for such miniatures is given in Richard Cosway's portrait of *Perdita Robinson, c.*1785, with its original fine heart-shaped enamel and ruby pendant (catalogue no. 29). The wearing of pendants is clearly illustrated in the miniature of an *Unknown Lady* by Hobday of 1797, at Kenwood (illustration 9), where it is suspended from a short choker but the setting is less ornate. A slightly longer necklace can be seen upon *A Portrait of a Lady* by Thomas Hazelhurst (location unknown, illustrated Foskett 1964, no. 396, plate 396) where a miniature of the sitter's husband can be clearly seen suspended within the centre of her cleavage. Andrew Plimer's example, *c.*1785-70, of a lady wearing a miniature with a more ornate pearl necklace can be seen in the current exhibition (catalogue no. 60). The miniature was normally worn on a longer chain, as depicted in the portrait of *Lady Jane James* by von Breda of 1794 (Sotheby's sale rooms 1945), and in numerous romantic portraits such as *Lady Elizabeth Foster* by Angelica Kauffmann of 1786, and *Mrs Crouch* by Romney at Kenwood (illustration 13). The royal family continued to wear miniatures, and Queen Charlotte's granddaughter *Princess Charlotte Augusta* is shown in the Holburne miniature by Rochard displaying a miniature of her fiancé Leopold of Saxe-Coburg-Saarfeld on a double gold necklace (illustration 10). This miniature was painted to celebrate the princess's engagement in 1815. The marriage was a happy one, but lasted for only one year. The princess died in childbirth in 1817 and her grieving grandmother, Queen Charlotte, who was in Bath at the time taking the waters, was required to cut short her visit and return to Windsor. The miniature continued to be favoured by the monarchy and when Queen Victoria married Prince Albert she gave each of her bridesmaids an enamel miniature of herself by Henry Pierce Bone, set in a gold bracelet. An example in the Duke of Norfolk's collection dated 1843 was presented to Mary Fitzalan Howard, daughter of the 1st Duke. Queen Victoria had all her children painted in miniature and one of the most charming nineteenth-century images is that of *Victoria, Princess Royal* as a child by the miniaturist Guglielmo Faija after John Lucas (Royal Collection). Princess Victoria is seen holding a miniature set in pearls of her beloved father, Prince Albert. A charming gold and blue enamel bracelet (now at Hagley Hall) inset with miniatures of Queen Victoria's five eldest children by Ross was presented to Lady Sarah Spencer on her retirement as their governess as a commemorative gift.

[10]
Princess Charlotte Augusta of Wales
Simon Jacques Rochard, Miniature, 1815
Holburne Museum, Bath

[11]
A Woman in Love (also called Peg Woffington)
Philip Mercier, circa 1735
The Garrick Club, London
Photograph Courtesy of the Paul Mellon Centre, London

The Romantic Image

As the eighteenth century progressed, so the trend towards romantic sensibility developed and the miniature took on an almost devotional anecdotal role. In numerous large oil paintings, such as Philip Mercier's portrait of *A Woman in Love*, sometimes called *Peg Woffington*, in the Garrick Club, miniatures provide the focus of interest (illustration 11). Here, in this early eighteenth century painting, a contemplative young woman gazes down upon the image of her suitor which she holds in her hand. Even her black dog in the background appears to share her emotion. Another Philip Mercier portrait at Marble Hill House, entitled *The Letter Writer*, and painted *c.*1738, shows a similar young lady writing a letter to her sweetheart with his tiny image propped up against her writing box. Presumably the attachment is a secret one for a strange character behind appears surprised by her activity. A romantic continuation of this theme can be found in Lethbridge's cabinet miniature on ivory entitled *The Miniature* (illustration 12). It shows a lady with, in one hand, a letter from her loved one, and in the other an open miniature case. She gazes intently upon the image therein, as does her black servant. Her bonnet has been casually thrown upon her chair as if she had just entered the room and opened the missive. On the reverse of the miniature are inscribed the following lines:

When Memory, chill'd by absence, shall decay,
And love's impression seems to wear away,
O! may this sketch with more than mimic art,
Recall the living Portrait to your heart,
Save an affection threatening to decline
And whilst, it pleads my faith, recover thine.

In 1787 George Romney portrayed the beautiful actress and singer *Mrs Crouch* for her husband, Lieutenant Crouch of the Royal Navy. This painting is now at Kenwood (illustration 13). Her husband's absence is alluded to by the boat at sea, far in the distance, whilst she is portrayed by a rock to symbolise constancy, wearing his miniature on a necklace. She draws the necklace to her bosom rather dramatically. Unfortunately for Lieutenant Crouch, in the case of his wife out of sight was out of mind and constancy thrown to the wind, as she was soon involved in a long-lasting affair with the charming Irish tenor Michael Kelly! Perhaps the most sentimental of all these paintings was Francis Danby's early nineteenth-century *Disappointed Love*, exhibited at the Royal Academy in 1821 and now in the Victoria and Albert Museum (FA 65). In this a weeping girl is portrayed on a river bank, her face concealed in her lap: the portrait image of her faithless lover lies on the bank beside her, and his letters torn to pieces are strewn in the river.

It was not always male sweethearts who were the subject of such paintings. The portrait by Angelica Kauffmann at Ickworth, mentioned above, shows *Lady Elizabeth Foster* wearing the 'beloved medallion' of her friend Georgiana, Duchess of Devonshire, and in Richard Cosway's portrait of *Mrs Joseph Smith* (Huntington Library, California) the sitter is clearly distressed after reading a letter from a female companion far away. In another Cosway oil painting, at Harewood House, *Mrs Scott* is shown presenting her daughter Henrietta, later Duchess of Portland, with her own miniature by the artist. That miniature survives in a private collection and provides the basis for the features of the later Harewood painting (see Lloyd 1995, no. 61).

The Miniature in Contemporary Literature

Early nineteenth-century literature very much reflects the importance that miniatures still maintained in middle- and upper-class life. The sending back of a miniature at the ending of an engagement was commonplace in England and abroad, as described in Tolstoy's *War and Peace* (published 1869): Andrei Bolkonski returns the letters together with the miniature of his fiancée, Countess Natasha Rostov, after she breaks off their engagement. There are fine miniatures of the Russian royal family represented in this exhibition (catalogue no. 55). In Jane Austen's novels there are a number of examples of the role of miniatures in polite society. In *Sense and Sensibility*, published in 1811, Lucy Ferrars, while trying to convince poor Elinor Dashwood that she has been secretly engaged to Edward Ferrars for four years, produces from her pocket a miniature and says to her potential rival:

> *'To prevent the possibility of a mistake, be so good as to look at this face. It does not do him justice to be sure, but yet, I think you cannot be deceived as to the person it was drew for.'*

Elinor is forced to acknowledge the likeness, and Lucy continues:

> *'I have never been able to give him my picture in return, which I am very much vexed at for he has always been so anxious to get it! But I am determined to sit for it at the very first opportunity.'*

When the engagement is broken her letters are burnt and the miniature returned. Another poignant moment occurs in *Persuasian*, published posthumously in 1818. At the end of the novel when all the characters come together in Bath, Captain Harville strikes up a conversation with Anne Elliot within hearing of her suitor Captain Wentworth. He shows Anne a miniature of his friend Captain Benwick and explains that Benwick's likeness was *'drawn at the Cape. He met there with a clever young German artist, and in compliance with a promise to my poor sister, sat to him and was bringing it home for her'.*

In the meantime Harville's sister had died, and Captain Benwick is now engaged to Louisa Musgrove. Harville explains that Benwick has charged him with 'getting the miniature properly set for another'. From this insensitive request springs a discussion between Harville and Anne about the relative constancy of men and women in love: the great theme of the novel. While the heartless Benwick may have too quickly forgotten his dead fiancée, many in the late eighteenth and early nineteenth centuries still attached a great deal of sentimentality to the miniature, especially when it represented a dear departed loved one. The role of miniatures as mourning tokens was also explored in Thackeray's *Vanity Fair.* Although published in 1847, it is of course set in the years before and after the Battle of Waterloo. At the very end of the novel, when the seemingly heartless Becky finally goes to Amelia to inform her of the truth concerning her dead husband, whom she had mourned for fifteen years, she finds her in her private apartment 'in the company of her miniatures and in a most melancholy and nervous condition'. Becky puts the case to Amelia that Dobbin would make an excellent husband, but the distraught widow explains that she has tried to put thoughts of her lost love aside, bewailing the fact that she could not forget, and she looks up at his portrait miniature. At this gesture Becky very irreverently exclaims of the dead husband:

'Couldn't forget him! That selfish humbug, that low-bred Cockney dandy, that padded booby, who had neither wit, nor manners, nor heart.'

Literature did not just dwell upon the miniature as a lover's token. The gentle young Dorothea in George Eliot's *Middlemarch* of 1871 noted, as she was shown her fiancé's home, that there were images of his forebears, 'miniatures of ladies and gentlemen with powdered hair hanging in a group'. No longer were such items kept just in the connoisseur's cabinet: they were now part of the family history and on general display.

India and the Miniature

In Thackery's *Vanity Fair* it is revealed that Becky also has a miniature hanging in her room which is an image of Jos, Amelia's brother and her first admirer. Beside it was a cabinet miniature, painted in India, of a gentleman riding an elephant. Jos had made his money in India and Dobbin had served there in the army. In the late eighteenth century the growth of the expatriate community in India provided numerous opportunities for the miniaturists to paint likenesses to be sent to loved ones back in

[12]
The Miniature
William Lethbridge
Present location unknown
(Photograph courtesy of Sotheby's)

[13]
Mrs Crouch (Anna Maria Phillips)
George Romney, 1787
The Iveagh Bequest, Kenwood
(English Heritage)

England. Both John Smart and Ozias Humphry spent periods of time in India. Smart was more financially successful than Humphry, who at one point was owed seven months' work by one Nawab. Robert Home was among the next generation of artists to trek out to India. He was appointed Court Painter to the Nawab of Oudh in 1814 and lived in Lucknow for thirteen years. He portrayed General Sir Edward Paget during his time in India from 1823 to 1825 (National Portrait Gallery (3247), illustration 14). Paget was presented on his arrival in India with a miniature of Ghazi-ud-din, King of Oudh. He wrote to his wife:

> *I dined with the King yesterday, he placed his portrait, set in a double row of diamonds and suspended by a double row of pearls round my neck, and begged I would wear it amongst my other decorations.*

The miniature of the king may have been by Home himself, although he was not officially employed as his miniature painter. Paget was painted by Home in a full-scale portrait which is now in the Asiatic Society of Bengal, Calcutta. It was commissioned by the king. This miniature copy appears to be after the large-scale painting and intended for Paget to keep as a memento of his visit.

In 1800 Charles Hayter portrayed a young boy who was the son of a purser in the service of the East India Company. This charming blond-haired child is shown in naval attire, popular at the time as a school uniform which suggests he may have been leaving home for school (V & A P23–1923). In one hand he holds a miniature and with the other gestures towards his mother and sisters (illustration 15). That miniature is also in the Victoria and Albert Museum (P24–1923) and is signed and dated by Hayter, London 1800. The sitters have not been firmly identified, but it is probable that the mother was returning to India, leaving her young son behind at school. Represented in the current exhibition is a miniature by Collins of *General Champneys* who served in the East India Company (catalogue no. 84). He later transferred to administration in 1784, working in Madras. As far as is known Collins never went to India and must have painted the General when he was on leave.

Miniatures and their Settings

The reverse of a miniature was an ideal space for storing locks of hair to preserve the remembrance of a young child. Engleheart's charming miniature in this exhibition, *Girl in a Black Hat* (catalogue no. 46), is set in an ornate diamond paste-style frame and has a most elaborate hair setting in the reverse. Lovers also frequently exchanged locks of hair to be set in frames with their miniatures. A fine example in the exhibition can be seen in John Smart's *Portrait of a Peeress in White,* signed and dated 1775 (catalogue no. 24). This miniature has a superb original gold, pearl and

[14]
General Sir Edward Paget
Robert Home, Miniature, 1823
By Courtesy of the National Portrait Gallery, London

diamond-set frame and a most elaborate reverse of hair setting, and contrasts with the plainer setting of hair for men of the period, such as that at the reverse of Philip Jean's *Man in Brown* (catalogue no. 44). A more elaborate hair setting for a male is Engleheart's *Lord Mountjoy*, in a gold and blue enamel locket with pearls (catalogue no. 51). A typical example in the current exhibition is Andrew Plimer's *Lady in White*, where the lady is shown wearing a miniature of her sweetheart (catalogue no. 60). When it is turned over the reverse reveals plumes of different fair and brown hair, presumably belonging to the couple, tied together in a love knot to represent a sheaf of corn, symbolising constancy. The inclusion of hair in a miniature was adopted by the monarchy as well. The Prince of Wales, later George IV, and his morganatic wife, Mrs Fitzherbert, were both painted by Cosway with borders of their plaited hair about them (Lloyd 1995, nos. 58 and 59). There also exists in the Victoria and Albert Museum a silhouette set in a bracelet made of hair (P165–1922). Cosway specialised in another branch of miniature painting at this time which detailed the sitter's eye or mouth. Probably the most famous example of this was *Mrs Fitzherbert's Eye* in a pearl crest-shaped setting, painted for the Prince of Wales in 1785.

The Royal Family continued to wear miniatures and to collect them. Queen Victoria had miniatures painted of her children and she also had the royal collection of miniatures reframed and catalogued. After the invention of photography in 1839 miniature painting had inevitably to resign its monopoly of the small reproduction of the face. As Katherine Coombs has pointed out, the lady in John Everett Millais' *Yes and No* of 1871 holds not the traditional miniature, but instead a *carte de visite* of her lover (Yale Centre for British Art). In spite of the fact that miniatures were being popularly supplanted by photography, some very fine nineteenth-century miniatures still exist. A good example is the portrait of *William Holman Hunt* by Edward Robert Hughes (catalogue no. 103), painted in the late 1880s, which was commissioned by his widow after the *Self Portrait* in the Uffizi (copy in the Athenaeum Club). The superb quality of this miniature, in its high Victorian jewelled setting, demonstrates that miniatures still played a part in the mourning process, even at the end of the nineteenth century. Many miniatures have been removed from their original jewelled settings, as these were often more valuable than the works themselves. The large number of original settings to be seen in this exhibition is unique and a testimony to this Collector's very discerning eye.

It is hoped that this survey of the historical and social role the miniature played from the sixteenth century until the nineteenth century will have given visitors to the exhibition an insight into the original functions of these intimate, poetic and portable portraits.

[15]
A Boy, the son of a purser in the East India Company
Charles Hayter, Miniature, circa 1800
The Victoria and Albert Museum, London

[16]
Unknown Woman and Two Children
Charles Hayter, Miniature, dated 1800
The Victoria and Albert Museum, London

A Private Collection of Miniatures

Richard Walker

Apart from the Jackdaw of Rheims, collecting is a human addiction. It began with Adam and Eve, who collected living creatures and gave them names. Thereafter people collected things of beauty. 'A thing of beauty is a joy for ever', and perhaps also an antidote to disaster, illness, senescence and other weaknesses. Adam knew nothing of old age and had no cause to dread it, but his children and grandchildren became aware all too soon and quickly realised that a thing of beauty possesses not only beauty but also something of eternal youth. I wonder if that is the motive behind this strange compulsion.

Charles Lamb, in his magical essay 'My Relations', said of his cousin James Elia, 'It does me good, on some fine May morning, to see him marching in a quite opposite direction, with a jolly handsome presence and a shining sanguine face that indicates some purchase in his eye – a Claude – or a Hobbema – for much of his enviable leisure is consumed at Christie's or Phillips . . .'. Is this an unfair account of our Collector? At the age of sixteen he made his first purchase – a portrait of a young woman hanging on the wall of a Hampstead restaurant. At twenty-four he blued his entire Post Office savings on a Romney oil of Lady Hamilton. An early start at miniature collecting came to grief in a burglary; and it was more galling to see his beloved little objects reappearing at auction at hopelessly increased prices. This Collection is the second edition, so to speak, and has been formed with the help of Mr David Lavender, a fellow tennis player and miniature enthusiast.

Collecting miniatures is a special refinement of the compulsion. It began in France at the court of François I, moved rapidly to England under Henry VIII, and became firmly established as an art in which Britain excelled, under Queen Elizabeth and her 'special conyng paynter' Nicholas Hilliard and his star pupil, Isaac Oliver. Works by Hilliard are beyond the means of most private collectors today, but this Collection has a Hilliard portrait of a man (catalogue no. 1) in which, though the eyes and flesh colours have faded, the fair hair and beard are exquisitely delineated with Hilliard's characteristic precision; and two authentic miniatures by Isaac Oliver (catalogue nos. 2 and 3). The second is of special interest. It belongs to a group of portraits of 'Young Women with Flowing Hair', a fashion which suggested virginity and was begun by Queen Elizabeth herself with a Hilliard portrait of about 1590. No. 3

shows Lady Dorothy Percy in 1614, on the eve of her clandestine marriage to the Earl of Leicester. Several versions are known, the original probably that in the Rijksmuseum (on loan to the Mauritshuis), where it was formerly called Lady Arabella Stuart but has lately been demoted to 'Lady with Flowing Hair'. So the identification with Lady Dorothy is specially satisfactory.

The Collection continues into the seventeenth century with an extremely interesting portrait by Cornelius Johnson, clearly signed and dated 1628, of a middle-aged man, possibly a nobleman or equerry at the Court of Charles I. Johnson was well known in the 1620s and 1630s as a painter of full-scale oil portraits and is now gradually becoming familiar as a skilful miniaturist; a considerable corpus of his miniatures is being documented. A much later portrait, attributed to a follower of Johnson and dated to about 1650, was given to the Holburne Museum in 1938 (illustration 17). Other notable seventeenth-century miniatures are the portrait of Lord Alington by the Polish miniaturist Franciszek Smiadecki, a very unusual portrait by the Dutchman Caspar Netscher, and one of several miniatures of the young Charles II by David Des Granges, probably painted during the King's exile in Holland and inscribed with the royal cypher CRII. The seventeenth-century section sadly has no Samuel Cooper, but has a striking portrait (catalogue no. 5) attributed to his less well-known brother, Alexander, and concludes with a splendid plumbago drawing by Robert White (catalogue no. 13), which complements the Holburne Museum's justly renowned collection of slightly later drawings by Thomas Foster, all collected by Sir William Holburne before 1865 when they appeared at the 'Special Exhibition of Portrait Miniatures' at South Kensington.

The Collection is strongest when we turn to the eighteenth-century miniatures. It begins with an unusual portrait attributed to Hyacinth Rigaud, a fashionable Parisian portrait painter not usually known as a miniaturist (catalogue no. 14). It is painted with delicacy and precision and, if not by the Master himself, is probably a copy of one of his full-scale oils of about 1710.

A particularly striking miniature is the Bernard Lens portrait of the artist John Wootton, aged about forty (catalogue no. 15). Very few portraits of this distinguished horse-painter are known, so this image will be of the greatest interest, and not only to students of racing iconography. It shows him informally dressed and with a sidelong glance that suggests an artist at work in his studio – or even the stable-yard.

Two good miniatures by John Barry and Jeremiah Meyer (catalogue nos. 21 and 22) lead to a group by John Smart, one of the most distinguished of eighteenth-century artists whose private life seems to have been far from exemplary but whose work as miniaturist and draughtsman is exquisite. The Collection has four early

[17]
Unknown Man
Follower of Cornelius Johnson
circa 1650
Holburne Museum of Art, Bath

[18]
George, Prince of Wales, later George IV
Richard Cosway
Holburne Museum of Art, Bath

Smart miniatures from the 1760s and 1770s, and two from 1801 demonstrating the high standard he maintained over many years (catalogue nos. 23–6, 80–81).

Smart's rival, Richard Cosway, is also well represented, with five miniatures ranging from the early 1770s to a charming portrait of Lady Elizabeth Bingham as a child in a large beribboned hat. Cosway's close association with the Prince of Wales is also reflected here. A very attractive portrait, in an unusual heart-shaped enamel and ruby frame, is almost certainly of his mistress, 'Perdita' Robinson (catalogue no. 29); and another of his morganatic wife, Mrs Fitzherbert, is an interesting derivation from the unfinished Gainsborough portrait which she detested because it ridiculed her long nose. The Prince's boon companion and Royal Groom, Colonel St Leger (nephew of the classic horse-race founder), was also painted by Gainsborough, as was the Prince himself; they exchanged portraits. A telling miniature of the Colonel, in scarlet coat and striped waistcoat, is by Michael Kean, better known as a director and leading spirit of the Crown Derby porcelain firm but also clearly an extremely talented miniature painter. Cosway's sketchy portrait of the Prince was an early acquisition for the Museum by Sir William Holburne (illustration 18).

The brothers Joseph and Abraham Daniel worked in Bristol and Bath as particularly accomplished miniaturists. The Collection has four works attributed to them, including the portrait of a child, possibly Princess Charlotte, the Prince Regent's daughter, and a fine portrait of an officer in the London and Westminster Light Horse regiment, of about 1795. This makes an interesting comparison with the Holburne Museum's 'Unknown Man' of *c.* 1790 (illustration 19).

Philip Jean, a Channel Islands man who served for a time in the navy under Rodney, turned to miniature painting and exhibited at the Royal Academy from 1787 to 1802, when he died in Hampstead. The Collection has three examples, of which no. 42, *Lady in White and Violet*, is a striking whole-length, comparable to Jean's *Dominic Serres* in the National Portrait Gallery (illustration 20).

The Collection is strong in miniatures by George Engleheart, one of the most distinguished of late Georgian portraitists. His best period, from about 1780 to 1795, is well represented. A typical example is catalogue no. 46, the little girl in a dashing black hat. Curiously enough the Holburne Museum itself has no Engleheart miniatures. Engleheart's sitter-book (the Fee Book) is still in the family possession, and it is particularly rewarding to be able to identify and date a number of his miniatures here.

Foreign artists are not much in evidence. The Rigaud portrait has already been mentioned. There is a typical Nattier of Madame de Pompadour holding an alluring chain of flowers and wearing a dress of the famous 'Nattier blue'. The Russian royal family appear in a group of seven, attributed to Jean-Louis Voille, showing the Empress Maria Feodorovna surrounded by six of her children (catalogue no. 55). She

[19]
Unknown Man
Joseph Daniel
circa 1790
Holburne Museum of Art, Bath

[20]
Dominic Serres
Philip Jean
National Portrait Gallery

appears again in catalogue no. 82, as a widow wearing a miniature of Paul I, confirming Dr Sumner's original and interesting thesis on the function of mourning miniatures (see p. 16). One of the innumerable miniatures of Napoleon, by Isabey, is here dated 1811 and shows the arch-villain in National Guard uniform and the Legion of Honour. Prince Achille Murat, son of Napoleon's cavalry commander, is represented here by Nicolas Dun (catalogue no. 99) as a young man shortly before his departure to the United States to take up American citizenship.

Characteristic works are here by John Bogle, Plimer, Crosse, and Edridge; and a penetrating portrait of an unknown man, *Man in Dark Blue* (catalogue no. 72), by the Scottish artist Archibald Skirving, is signed and dated 1798, shortly before he abandoned miniature painting for the less exacting pastel work. This is one of the star turns in the current Skirving exhibition at the Scottish National Portrait Gallery, where the long-neglected Skirving is credited with his rightful place alongside Ramsay and Raeburn.

Two miniatures by William Wood, of William Rush and his wife (catalogue nos. 73–4), are fully documented in Wood's sitter-book which contains absorbing details of colour, size, clothes, expression, and sometimes exquisitely neat tracings in red ink of the miniature itself. Mrs Rush, for instance, has 'an open turban and an averted dark eye', and her husband 'a sunburnt but fair complexion'.

The Collection ends in the nineteenth century with works by Collins, Hargreaves, Freeze, Chinnery, and Chalon, whose portrait of the Princess Charlotte Augusta (catalogue no. 94), when compared with the Holburne Museum Rochard of her (illustration 10), demonstrates how her hair mysteriously changes from the Hanoverian flax of her childhood and youth to a rich chestnut brown! Finally, there is a miniature copy of Holman Hunt's self-portrait in Florence, painted in 1880 and presented to the Guild of St Luke to join its unique collection of artists' self-portraits stretching back to the Renaissance. The copy, set in a filigree frame and bought from Holman Hunt's housekeeper, is probably by the artist's friend Edward Hughes, but could also be by his widow, Marion Edith, a talented artist herself, as we know from her granddaughter's enthralling book, *My Grandfather, His Wives and Loves.*

Among the many attractions of this distinguished collection of miniatures are the reverses of the lockets or cases. Many of these are shown here accompanying the illustration of the miniature itself. They are often of great beauty, set in blue glass, pearl and diamond borders, with enamelled or opalescent backgrounds, gold monogrammed initials, and with tresses of the sitters' hair, sometimes plaited with fair and dark hair entwined in touching unison. These reverses form an epilogue to a collection which celebrates a form of art specially British and in which British artists have excelled from the days of Henry VIII to Queen Victoria.

Contents of the Catalogue

16th Century

1. Nicholas Hilliard, *c.* 1590

17th Century

2–3. Isaac Oliver, *c.* 1600, *c.* 1615

4. British or Dutch School, 1620–25

5. Alexander Cooper, *c.* 1640

6–7. Cornelius Johnson, 1628, *c.* 1645

8. French School, 1660–70

9. Franciszek Smiadecki, *c.* 1665

10. Caspar Netscher, *c.* 1670

11. David Des Granges, *c.* 1655

12. Peter Cross, *c.* 1678

13. Robert White, *c.* 1680

Early 18th Century

14. Hyacinthe Rigaud, *c.* 1710

15. Bernard Lens, *c.* 1720

16. Arthur Devis, 1747

Late 18th Century

17. J.-M. Nattier, *c.* 1758

18. J.-B. Massé, *c.* 1760

19. French School, *c.* 1775

20. British School, *c.* 1755–9

21. John Barry, *c.* 1795

22. Jeremiah Meyer, *c.* 1775

23–6. John Smart, 1768–80

27–35. Richard Cosway, 1770–1805

36–8. Abraham Daniel, 1780–99

39. Joseph Daniel, *c.* 1795

40. 'V', *c.* 1780

41. Thomas Day, *c.* 1785

42–4. Philip Jean, *c.* 1785–90

45–54. George Engleheart, 1780–1810

55. J.-L. Voille, 1788

56. John Bogle, 1789

57–8. Horace Hone, 1790–95

59–60. Andrew Plimer, 1785–90

61. Michael Kean, *c.* 1785

62. L.-M. Sicardi, 1790

63. Pierre Rouvier, *c.* 1790

64. Richard Crosse, *c.* 1790

65. Henry Jacob Burch, 1791

66. Charles Shirreff, 1794

67. François Ferrière, *c.* 1795

68–9. Henry Edridge, 1795–1800

70. Sir William Beechey (after), *c.* 1797

71. Mathias Finucane, *c.* 1798

72. Archibald Skirving, 1798

73–4. William Wood, 1796–8

75–9. George Engleheart, 1795–1802

19th Century

80–81. John Smart, 1801

82–3. Franz Kügelgen, 1789–1801

84. Richard Collins, *c.* 1805

85–8. Thomas Hargreaves, 1807–12

89. L.-A. Collas, *c.* 1810

90. J.-B. Isabey, 1811

91. N. Freese, *c.* 1810

92. George Chinnery, *c.* 1810

93–4. Alfred Edward Chalon, 1815–17

95. J.C.D. Engleheart, 1815–25

96. John Wright, 1816

97–8. Henri Grevedon, 1818

99. Nicolas François Dun, *c.* 1820

100. M.M. Daffinger, *c.* 1821

101–2. Andrew Plimer, *c.* 1829

103. Edward Robert Hughes, *c.* 1880

The Catalogue

Note on the Catalogue

Measurements of the miniatures, excluding the frames, are given in millimetres, followed by inches in brackets, height before width.

HS = head and shoulders HL = half-length
TQL = threequarter-length WL = whole-length

I

Nicholas Hilliard, 1547–1619

Man with Fair Hair and Beard, c. 1590

Watercolour on vellum backed with ivory,
oval 51 × 42 mm (2 × 1 5/8 in),
uninscribed.

HS to left, black doublet, high white ruff; pale grey eyes, fair beard and moustache, curly fair hair, aged about 45; plain blue background.
Oval pearwood frame with ivory inset and back.

Collection: private collection no. 101.

Nicholas Hilliard, generally recognised as one of the most distinguished miniaturists of all time, settled himself at the Court of Queen Elizabeth I, painted portraits of many of the shining stars surrounding her throne, such as the Earl of Essex, Sir Walter Raleigh and Sir Francis Drake, and indeed was one of the few artists allowed the royal warrant to paint Gloriana herself. The identity of the *Man with Fair Hair and Beard* has not yet been established. He bears some resemblance to the Hilliard miniature of Lord Howard of Effingham, hero of the Armada campaign, in the National Maritime Museum, and may conceivably be a sketch for an earlier portrait of him, though this is by no means certain.

2

Isaac Oliver, *c.* 1565–1617

Portrait of a Man said to be Robert Devereux, 2nd Earl of Essex, c. 1600

Watercolour on vellum,
oval 44 × 37 mm (1¾ × 1½ in),
uninscribed.

HS facing, black doublet, white lawn collar with lace border and ruff, narrow ribbon of the Garter; greenish-brown eyes, brownish-red beard, aged about 30; dark red background with restored gold border.
Original pale blue enamel locket.

Exhibition: 'Special Exhibition of Portrait Miniatures', South Kensington Museum, 1865 (1182), as by Peter Oliver and lent by the Countess of Caledon.
Literature: Williamson 1906, I, no. 49; Strong 1969, pp. 116–17; Strong 1984, pp. 161–2.
Collections: C.F. Huth; J. Pierpont Morgan, sold Christie's 24–7 June 1935 (174); bought from the Howell family; private collection no. 91.

Isaac Oliver was born probably in France or Switzerland, came to England as a child with his Huguenot father in about 1568, studied under Nicholas Hilliard and indeed, by the date of this miniature, had become his most formidable rival at the Court of Queen Elizabeth. He continued working well into the next reign and was a great favourite with James I's Queen, Anne of Denmark, and their eldest son, Henry Frederick, Prince of Wales.

Robert Devereux was a favourite of Queen Elizabeth, whom he displeased by marrying Frances, widow of Sir Philip Sidney. He was executed in 1601. He was a staunch patron of Isaac Oliver, and the original of this miniature is probably a whole-length portrait, once in Charles I's collection and now privately owned (reproduced in Strong 1984, fig. 207). He painted several versions and variants of the head and shoulders – in the Royal Collection, the National Portrait Gallery, and at Burghley House, Chatsworth and Manchester Art Gallery (on loan from Lord Derby). This portrait appears to be, though very like Essex, considerably later, *c.* 1605, in fact after the execution, and may be wrongly identified. The fullest account of the Essex iconography is in D. Piper, *Burlington Magazine 99* (1957), where this miniature is not admitted.

3

Isaac Oliver, *c.*1565–1617

Dorothy, Countess of Leicester, c. 1615

Watercolour on vellum stuck to a playing card (two of clubs),
rectangle 52 × 41 mm (2⅛ × 1⅝ in),
signed upper right: *I O*, and inscribed on reverse (perhaps in a 17th-century hand):
La: Dorothy Percy / afterwards / Countesse of Leycister

HS to left, embroidered dress, red shawl over her right shoulder, pearl necklace,
falling ruff; light brown eyes, fair hair adorned with a flowery wreath.
19th-century silver frame with rope motif.

Exhibition: 'Chefs d'Œuvre de la miniature et de la gouache', Geneva, 1956 (32).
Literature: Finston 1981, II, p. 119, for the Rijksmuseum variant.
Collections: bought privately from Germany; private collection no. 88.

The miniature is one of several portraits, of varying quality, of young women with flowing hair, a motif indicating purity; they sometimes show the arms crossed, suggesting faithfulness. The idea was originated by Nicholas Hilliard in a famous portrait of Queen Elizabeth as 'Stella Britanniae' of about 1600 (Victoria and Albert Museum). A variant in the Rijksmuseum has previously been identified with Lady Arabella Stuart but this has lately been changed to 'Lady with Flowing Hair'. Another, without the floral wreath but with the same falling ruff, is at Sherborne Castle, called possibly Venetia Stanley, Lady Digby. Lady Dorothy is shown here in 1614/15, on the eve of her clandestine marriage to Lord Robert Sydney, later Earl of Leicester.

4

British or Dutch School, early 17th century

Man in a Buff Jerkin, 1620–25

Oil on copper,
oval 59 × 44 mm ($2^1/_4$ × $1^3/_4$ in),
uninscribed.

HS to right in a buff leather jerkin, broad green sash over his right shoulder, falling white collar-ruff; hazel eyes, light brown hair, upturned moustache, aged about 40. Plain brown background. Ebonised wood frame.

Collection: private collection no. 44.

A good example of a type of seventeenth-century miniature, painted in oils on copper or brass often cut from metal ammunition boxes. They were more popular on the continent, especially in Holland and Italy, than in England where the medium favoured was watercolour or gouache on vellum giving a more translucent effect. Oil miniatures tend to be coarse in technique and never attain the delicacy of touch achieved by watercolour. A fine collection of oil miniatures is at Stourhead in Wiltshire, mostly copies of full-scale portraits.

The identity of this sitter is unknown at present. He appears to be a bluff military character, expensively dressed in the clothes of the early 1620s. His swashbuckling air suggests a Dutchman, painted in the manner of van Miereveld.

5

Alexander Cooper, 1609–*c.* 1660

Gaston d'Orléans, c. 1640

Watercolour on vellum,
oval 50 × 41 mm (2 × 1⅝ in),
uninscribed.
HS to right, open shirt with falling lace collar, pearl ear-ring; hazel eyes, long brown wavy hair, light brown moustache; plain buff background darker to left.
Modern silver frame with spiral cresting.

Collection: private collection no. 102.

Alexander Cooper, elder brother of the more famous miniaturist Samuel Cooper, spent most of his working life in northern Europe, especially Holland and Sweden. This striking portrait was probably painted in France. Gaston d'Orléans, son of Henri IV and younger brother of Louis XIII, was well known for the eccentricity of his clothes which would certainly match the unusual shirt worn by the figure in this miniature. Van Dyck's whole-length portrait of Gaston in the Musée Condé, Chantilly, shows a darker man with a more oval face and pointed chin.

6

Cornelius Johnson, 1593–1661

Man in a White Ruff, 1628

Oil on copper,
oval 89 × 69 mm (3½ × 2¾ in),
signed and dated lower right: *CJ / 1628.*

HS to right in a dark coat, falling ruff with two tassels; dark grey eyes, scanty brown hair, thick brown beard and moustache, aged 40–50; plain dark background. Plain silver gilt locket.

Exhibition: British Portrait Exhibition, Edinburgh, 1965, no. 45, lent by Mrs Blofeld.
Collections: acquired from the Blofeld family in 1996; private collection no. 9.

7

Attributed to Cornelius Johnson

Young Man in Black, c. 1645

Oil on copper,
oval 51 × 42 mm (2 × 1⅝ in),
uninscribed.

HS to right, black coat, square falling collar with tassel; grey eyes, long brown hair with centre parting, long turned-up nose, sensuous lips, aged about 20; plain brown background.
Plain gun-metal locket.

Collections: formerly belonging to Dr G.C. Williamson and possibly sold Sotheby's 28 February 1945 (40); private collection no. 10.

Cornelius Johnson, born in London but probably trained in Holland, is better known as a painter of portraits in full scale rather than as a miniaturist. However, a small and ever-growing corpus of oil miniatures by him is becoming known, and it is specially rewarding to study the *Man in a White Ruff* (no. 6), which is clearly signed and dated 1628, and has the serene and rather diffident expression characteristic of Johnson's work. The *Young Man in Black* is less certain and, if it is by Johnson, is probably after 1643 when he retired to Holland because of his wife's terror of the Civil War.

8

French School, late 17th century

Portrait of a Man, c. 1660–70

Oil on card,
oval 65 × 53 mm (2½ × 2⅛ in),
uninscribed.

HS to right, steel cuirass under red cloak, white lace collar, large blue silk bow tie; dark blue eyes, long curly brown hair, moustache and goatee beard, aged 40–50; plain brown background.
Original pewter frame with scored leather backing.

Collection: private collection no. 75.

9

Franciszek Smiadecki, late 17th century

Portrait of Lord Alington, c. 1665

Oil on copper on vellum,
oval 43 × 37 mm (1⅝ × 1½ in) sight size,
uninscribed.

HS slightly to left, dark blue coat, yellow waistcoat, white unbuttoned shirt; hazel eyes, young podgy face, coarse nose, red lips, aged about 25; plain dark background.
Pearwood frame with brass inset; numeral 5 on the exposed vellum back.

Collection: private collection no. 42.

Smiadecki, of Polish or Russian origin, is believed to have been taught the art of miniature painting in Sweden by one of the Cooper brothers. His miniatures were usually painted in oils on copper. William Alington (*c.*1635–84), soldier under the Holy Roman Emperor and Constable of the Tower of London, married Juliana, daughter of Lord Camden, in 1664, possibly the occasion for this miniature.

10

Caspar Netscher, 1635/6–1684

Lady in Yellow, c. 1670

Oil on copper,
oval 162 × 123 mm (6⅜ × 4⅞ in),
signed on the tablecloth: *Netscher.*

HL to right, head to left, bodice imitating a steel cuirass, yellow dress, blue cloak, pearl necklace, hands on table with a red cloth; brown eyes, pale face, red lips, head tilted sideways to left, serious expression, aged about 20; reddish brown curtain to left.
Fine carved wood frame.

Collection: private collection no. 64.

Netscher, brought up in Arnhem but working mainly in The Hague, is not normally known as a miniaturist. The Rijksmuseum, the Mauritshuis and the National Gallery, London, have genre, portrait and figure paintings by him, and this is possibly a small copy of one of his portraits.

11

David Des Granges, *c.* 1611–71/2

Charles II, c. 1655

Watercolour on vellum,
oval 63 × 49 mm (2½ × 2 in),
inscribed to left with royal cypher in gold.

HS to left, in armour, falling lace collar with two tassels, Garter riband; brown eyes, long black hair with centre parting, slight moustache, aged about 25; plain grey background.
Original hinged sharkskin case.

Exhibition: 'The Monarchy in Important Miniatures from Elizabeth I to Queen Victoria', D.S Lavender Antiques, London, 1993 (34).
Collections: acquired from the Walpole family by D.S. Lavender Antiques; private collection no. 92.

Des Granges, of a Huguenot family but brought up in London, seems to have become attached to the young King Charles II when in exile in Holland, though copies by him are known of Hoskins's portrait of Prince Charles as a child in the late 1630s, and several versions are known of his excellent copy of the head in Hanneman's portrait of 1648. He was appointed His Majesty's Limner in Scotland in 1651. Charles II was born in 1630, and the relative immaturity of his features in this picture, despite the incipient moustache, suggests a date around 1650–55.

12

Peter Cross, *c.* 1645–1724

Carey, Countess of Peterborough, c. 1678

Watercolour on vellum,
oval 78 × 62 mm (3 × 2⅜ in),
uninscribed.

HL slightly to right, blue dress over a white blouse, gold and grey shawl; hazel eyes, dark hair over her left shoulder, pearl ear drop, aged 20–25; plain buff background.
Plain gilt metal locket with spiral crest.

Exhibition: this or a duplicate was in 'Portrait Miniatures', Burlington Fine Arts Club (1889).
Collections: acquired from the Blofeld family by D.S. Lavender Antiques; private collection no. 21.

Carey Fraser, daughter of Sir Alexander Fraser, Bt, physician to Charles II, married in about 1678 Charles, Viscount Mordaunt, later Earl of Peterborough. They were both under age and the wedding was held in secret. The portrait is close to a whole-length oil by Kneller, and, although here attributed to Peter Cross, is possibly a copy or adaptation by Christian Richter, painted early in the following century.

13

Robert White, 1645–1703

Portrait of a Man, c. 1680

Plumbago on vellum,
oval 49 × 39 mm (2 × 1½ in) sight size,
uninscribed.

HS to right, embroidered collar; long black rather untidy hair, low brow, heavy bulbous nose, long chin, smiling expression.
Turned ebonised wood frame.

Collection: private collection no. 51.

Robert White, together with his master, David Loggan, and Thomas Forster, are associated with the flowering of that delectable art of portrait drawing in pencil, then known as plumbago or graphite. They managed to endow their work with a special lustre due to the quality of the lead mined at Borrowdale in the Lake District. An unfinished plumbago portrait by Robert White of the ill-fated Duke of Monmouth is also in the Holburne Museum, where there is a specially interesting group of twelve identified portrait drawings by Thomas Forster.

14

Hyacinthe Rigaud, 1659–1743

Lady in Blue, c. 1710

Oil on copper,
oval 40 × 35 mm (1½ × 1⅜ in) sight size,
uninscribed.

HS to left, white dress embroidered with gold, blue cloak, pearl necklace; large blue eyes, brown hair, ear ring in her left ear, sensuous lips, aged 25–30; dark background.

Original gold locket in a black fish skin case, with coronets and different monogram initials on each side.

An unrelated French inscription in red ink on stiff paper forms the backing paper.

Collections: Dyson Perrins collection (920), sold Sotheby's 11 December 1958 and again 14 May 1959 (7), as 'English School *c.* 1700'; Blofeld family collection; private collection no. 11.

The miniature is clearly French in origin and is here attributed to Hyacinthe Rigaud, an eminently successful portrait painter in Paris during the first half of the eighteenth century but not generally known as a miniaturist; it certainly is very like his work in style and may be a copy of one of his full-scale portraits of about 1710.

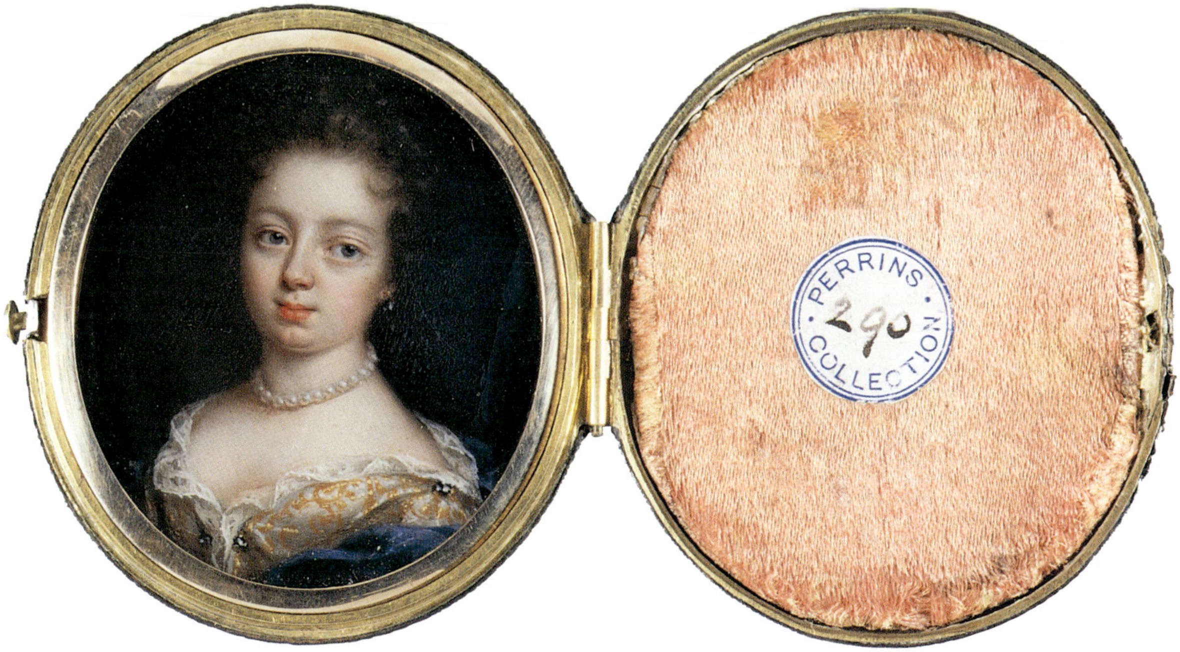
PERRINS
290
COLLECTION

15

Bernard Lens, 1682–1740

Portrait of John Wootton, c. 1720

Watercolour on ivory,
oval 81 × 60 mm (3¼ × 2⅜ in),
signed with gold monogram *BL*, and inscribed in ink on the polygonal mahogany backing: *Wootton the Portrait Painter*, and in a later hand: *Sr Peter Lilly.*

HS to right in a green coat, blue-grey shirt open at the neck; pale grey eyes, pale face with greenish modelling, full wig, sidelong inquiring expression, aged 40–45. Brown pearwood contemporary frame.

Collections: Blofeld family; private collection no. 34.

Bernard Lens was in the third generation of a family of artists migrating to London probably from Germany. He was appointed Painter in Enamel to George I in 1723, no doubt because, the King's command of English being rudimentary, they were able to communicate easily. He continued in office under George II, but his main interest is the revolutionary introduction of ivory as a vehicle for miniature painting instead of vellum or card. This allows full scope to the transparency inherent in watercolour, the ivory itself sometimes showing through the pigment to provide further highlights.

Wootton (*c.*1678–1764) is here described as a portrait painter though he was mainly known as the painter of horses, sporting conversation pieces and occasional equestrian portraits of the English aristocracy. Not many portraits of him are known so this vivid image by Bernard Lens is something of a treasure. A self-portrait chalk drawing as a chubby young man is in the British Museum. He appears aged about fifty, in a group of artists and collectors, by Gavin Hamilton, in the National Portrait Gallery; and also by Gavin Hamilton, in a family group of 1736. So this perceptive portrait of the artist aged about forty, by a distinguished contemporary miniaturist, is of great interest.

16

Arthur Devis, *c.* **1711–87**

John Tennant, 1747

Watercolour on ivory,
oval 43 × 37 mm (1⅝ × 1½ in),
inscribed lower left: *Aetatis 25 / 1747*, and signed lower right: *ADevis ft.*

HL to left in a blue coat, grey-green waistcoat embroidered with gold, white necktie; hazel eyes, long dark hair, aged 25; plain buff background.
Gilt metal locket engraved with the Tennant coat of arms.

Collections: Tennant family; private collection no. 27.

Arthur Devis is more generally known as a painter of small-scale conversation pieces and neat, genteel single figures, so this miniature is of considerable interest. As with many artists of the time he liked to experiment with different media. Two comparable miniatures, painted in oil on copper, of himself and his wife Elizabeth, are in the Harris Museum and Art Gallery at Preston. Otherwise no miniatures by him are known at present.

John Tennant (1722–90) was born in Yorkshire, went up to St John's College, Cambridge, in 1739, and is recorded as Master of the Bench of the Middle Temple in 1779.

17

Jean-Marc Nattier, 1685–1766

Madame de Pompadour, c. 1758

Watercolour on ivory,
rectangle 52 × 73 mm (2⅛ × 2⅞ in),
uninscribed.

TQL to left, white dress, blue cloak, holding a lavish chain of flowers; blue eyes, powdered hair dressed with berries; trees and sky background.
Modern chased gold frame with claw back.

Collection: private collection no. 85.

Madame de Pompadour, the exquisitely beautiful favourite of Louis XV, was painted many times by Nattier, Boucher, Welper and Watteau. The head in this miniature is very like that in a Boucher portrait in the Alte Pinakothek, Munich, but the blue cloak and floral chain are unmistakable Nattier hallmarks, and this miniature is probably a copy of one of his full-size portraits.

18

Jean-Baptiste Massé, 1687–1767

Girl Blowing Bubbles, c. 1760

Watercolour on ivory,
rectangle 52 × 74 mm (2⅛ × 2⅞ in),
uninscribed.

TQL seated to left, soap bowl in left hand, bubble pipe upwards in right hand, square-cut patterned dress; blue eyes, long fair hair with pearls, aged about 8; window with lake and mountains in left background, red curtain and architecture to right.

Chased gold frame with claw back.

Collection: private collection no. 84.

Massé, born and died in Paris, painted portraits and miniatures for Cardinal Richelieu and Louis XV who appointed him 'garde des tableaux' in 1759. The *Girl Blowing Bubbles* was possibly intended for the lid of a box.

19

French School, late 18th century

Officer in Scarlet Uniform, c. 1775

Watercolour on ivory,
oval 35 × 28 mm ($1\frac{3}{8} \times 1\frac{1}{8}$ in),
uninscribed.

HS to right, head to left, scarlet uniform, steel cuirass, white sword-belt; brown eyes, short grey wig in queue, face strongly modelled with short blue-grey strokes, aged about 35; sky background, darker to left.
Plain modern oval gilt locket with engraved ellipses on back.

Collection: private collection no. 86.

Neither artist nor sitter is known at present. They could both be either British or French.

20

British School, mid 18th century

Major O'Connor, c. 1755–9

Watercolour on ivory,
oval 41 × 31 (1⅝ × 1¼ in),
uninscribed.

HS to left, scarlet uniform with white facings, black neckcloth, powdered hair in queue; blue eyes, long nose, pale face modelled with short bluish strokes, aged about 40; bluish-grey background.
Plain gilt metal locket with glazed reverse revealing an inscription in ink: *Major O'Connor / 46th Regiment / Killed at Quebec / – 1759.*

Collection: private collection no. 47.

The miniature was formerly attributed to Ozias Humphry (1741–1810), who would have been aged about 14 or 15 when the portrait was painted. If the identity with Major O'Connor is correct this is unlikely.

Major Connor
46th Regiment
Killed at Quebec
~1759~

21

John Barry, fl. 1784–1827

William Wyndham, c. 1795

Watercolour on ivory,
oval 63 × 50 mm (2½ × 2 in),
uninscribed.

HS to right, brown coat with silver buttons and powder on collar, yellow waistcoat, white bow tie; brown eyes, powdered wig, angular eyebrows, aged 30–35; sky background in neat striations.
Reframed in a plain reddish gold locket.

Literature: H.A. Wyndham, *A Family History 1688–1837,* 1950, p. 232.
Collection: private collection no. 43.

The miniature was formerly in a silver-gilt frame with spiral cresting and attributed to Andrew Plimer, but the characteristics of Barry's unmistakable style are clearly evident in this striking portrait, noticeably in the sharply angled eyebrows, sculptured lips, brownish vertical modelling, and massed treatment of the hair.

William Wyndham (1769–1841) married Laetitia Popham and had six sons; he served in the West Wiltshire Yeomanry. Miniatures of the Wyndham family of about this date are at Felbrigg Hall, Norfolk (National Trust).

22

Jeremiah Meyer, 1735–89

Man in Brown, c. 1775

Watercolour on ivory,
oval 56 × 45 mm (2¼ × 1¾ in),
uninscribed.

HS to right in a brown velvet coat, white neckcloth and lace cravat, possibly the Garter riband; light brown eyes, pale (faded) face, neat powdered wig in queue, aged about 25; sky background.
Plain gilt metal locket.

Collection: private collection no. 5.

Meyer came to England from Germany as a boy in about 1750. He was apprenticed to Zincke and enjoyed the patronage of George III for whom he painted a miniature to be sent to Princess Charlotte of Mecklenburg-Strelitz as an engagement present (see page 25). His work is easily recognisable from a number of mannerisms – fine linear modelling, opaque white in the highlights, protruding sculptured lips, sunk-back eyes. As has happened here, the flesh-tints often faded due to the fugitive composition of his red pigments.

23

John Smart, 1742/3–1811

Portrait of a Lady in Blue and Pink, 1768

Watercolour on ivory,
oval 42 × 34 mm (1⅝ × 1⅜ in),
signed and dated lower left: *J.S. 1768.*

HS to right, slashed blue dress with white frilly lace collar, pink shawl, pearl and ruby necklace; brown eyes, upswept brown hair with pearls, aged 40–50; sky background.
Plain gold locket.

Collections: Ernest Renton 1891; Charles E. Lees 1997; private collection no. 66.

24

John Smart, 1742/3–1811

Portrait of a Peeress in White, 1775

Watercolour on ivory,
oval 47 × 38 mm (1⅞ × 1½ in),
signed and dated lower left: *JS 1775.*

HS to left in a white dress, mauve ermine-edged robe; hazel eyes, brown hair with jewelled clips, highly coloured complexion, aged about 40; plain brown background.
Gold locket with pearl border and diamond crest, plaited brown hair in the back under a gold monogram *GF* or *JF.*

Collection: private collection no. 52.

John Smart is undoubtedly one of the most distinguished of British eighteenth-century miniaturists. Sir David Piper has perceptively described him as 'the most naturalistic of the 18th century miniature painters, who aimed above all at exactness of likeness, had no truck with the frills and graces, yet achieved a sparkling prettiness'. Even his rival Cosway considered Smart's work to be 'extremely like . . . certainly without any flattery'. He seems to have accomplished these effects by means of consummate draughtsmanship (many of his preliminary drawings survive), the use of clear brilliant colours which have not faded with the lapse of time, and a penetrating judgement of his sitters' characters. He also had the endearing habit of adding a signature and date to his miniatures. Examples of his work are in most collections, specially interesting groups being at Ickworth and Southside House, Wimbledon.

25

John Smart, 1742/3–1811

Portrait of a Man in Grey, 1779

Watercolour on ivory,
oval 45 × 36 mm (1¾ × 1⅜ in),
signed and dated lower left: *JS 1729.*

HS to right, grey coat edged with gold, green waistcoat, white neckcloth; brown eyes, ruddy face, short wig in queue, aged about 50–60; plain brown background. Plain gold locket with engraved rim.

Collection: private collection no. 46.

26

John Smart, 1742/3–1811

Portrait of a Man in Black, 1780

Watercolour on ivory,
oval 38 × 31 mm (1½ × 1¼ in),
signed and dated lower left: *JS 1780.*

HS to right, dark grey coat, white shirt and bow tie; short neat powdered wig, aged 55–60; plain grey background.
Gold bracelet locket with diamanté border.

Collection: private collection no. 59.

27

Richard Cosway, R.A., 1742–1821

Lady in White, 1770–75

Watercolour on ivory,
oval 59 × 46 mm (2⅜ × 1⅞ in),
uninscribed.

HL to right, low-cut white dress with frilly collar, pearl necklace; hazel eyes, long fair hair, smiling, aged about 20; sky background.
Gold locket with monogram on blue glass within a pale blue enamel border.

Collection: private collection no. 48.

28

Richard Cosway, R.A., 1742–1821

Portrait of Anne Sawbridge, c. 1775

Watercolour on ivory,
oval 41 × 35 mm (1⅝ × 1⅜ in),
uninscribed.

HS to right, white frilly dress, blue straps and matching blue hair ribbons; large blue eyes, long fair hair, vacuous expression, aged 25–30; sky background.
Plain gold locket.

Collection: private collection no. 23.

The sitter was Anne Stephenson, married in 1766 as his second wife to Alderman John Sawbridge, who was elected MP for Hythe in 1768 and for London in 1774, 1780, 1784 and 1790; he became Lord Mayor of London in 1775.

29

Richard Cosway, R.A., 1742–1821

'Perdita' Robinson, c. 1785
(possibly)

Watercolour on ivory,
cordate 20 × 17 mm (3/4 × 5/8 in),
uninscribed.

HS to right, white dress with pearls; brown eyes, powdered hair; sky background.
Original heart-shaped enamel and ruby frame.

Collection: private collection no. 93.

The sitter was Mary Robinson (1758–1800), actress and mistress of the Prince of Wales. She was painted by Gainsborough and Romney, and her magnificent portrait by Reynolds is at Waddesdon Manor.

Cosway's enormously popular reputation may be said to have depended largely on his life style, which was eccentric to say the least of it. He affected exotic clothing, claimed to have had sittings from the Virgin Mary, and lived in the house in Pall Mall known as the Temple of Health. His musical parties attracted the fashionable world and he was taken up by the Duchess of Devonshire, Mrs Fitzherbert and, through them, the Prince of Wales himself. They all fell for his style of painting their portraits with winsome smiles, huge melting eyes, a hectic flush, and a cheerful sky background painted with a brilliant azure. His painting was also technically highly skilful, and by brilliant modelling he was able to achieve a startling effect of the third dimension, and sometimes a work of art of great beauty.

30

Richard Cosway, R.A., 1742–1821

Mrs Phillipson, c. 1789

Watercolour on ivory,
oval 71 × 58 mm (2¾ × 2¼ in),
signed and dated on reverse, 1789.

HL to right, white dress, dark blue sash; huge brown eyes, long powdered hair to shoulders, strong shadow on her left cheek, sfumato lips, aged about 25; sky background.
Plain gold locket with plait of dark brown hair.

Collection: private collection no. 36.

This is possibly a case of mistaken identity. A Cosway portrait of Mrs Phillipson, found round the neck of General Richard Burton Phillipson who was killed in India in 1792, also had noticeably brown eyes and fair hair but appears to be of a different sitter (Edward Paine sale, Christie's, 20 March 1989, lot 130).

31

Richard Cosway, R.A., 1742–1821

Portrait of Mrs Fitzherbert, c. 1795

Watercolour on ivory,
oval 93 × 74 mm (3⅝ × 2⅞ in),
uninscribed.

HS to left, right hand to face, frilly yellow dress (faded), white bow under chin, white bonnet; brown eyes, long nose, long powdered hair, smiling expression; red curtain background.
Gold locket case engraved: *Mrs Fitzherbert.*

Collection: private collection no. 24.

The miniature is adapted from Gainsborough's half-length portrait of Mrs Fitzherbert, painted for the Prince of Wales in 1784 and now in San Francisco – a portrait which Mrs Fitzherbert disliked intensely because, she said, it exaggerated the length of her nose. Cosway would have had ample opportunity to copy the portrait; he and Gainsborough lived in the same house in Pall Mall.

32

Richard Cosway, R.A., 1742–1821

Major Henry Richmond Gale, 1790–95

Watercolour on ivory,
oval 51 × 39 mm (2 × 1½ in),
uninscribed.

HS to right, grey coat, white waistcoat, bow tie and shirt frill; brown eyes,
powdered hair in queue, aged about 30; sky background.
Gold frame with plaited hair, marcasite, beads and flowers on blue glass.

Collections: Commander Lyaddyll; L.H. Gilbert of Lisbon; Christie's 3 December 1963, 25 November 1987 (385); Walter and Gertrude Rappolt collection; private collection no. 89.

The sitter is believed to be Henry Richmond Gale, who joined the 7th Light Dragoons in 1780, captain in 20th Light Dragoons 1782, major 1783, colonel 1798, major-general 1805, lieutenant-general 1811; he died in 1814. It portrays him as a major, in civilian clothes.

33

Richard Cosway, R.A., 1742–1821

Lieutenant John Mackintosh, c. 1805

Watercolour on ivory,
oval 67 × 52 mm (2⅝ × 2⅛ in),
uninscribed.

HS to right in marine's uniform (scarlet with blue collar, epaulette and white sword belt); hazel eyes, fair hair in queue, aged about 19; cloudy sky background. Gold locket, with spray of hair held with gold wire and seed pearls on opalescent glass.

Literature: Army Lists and papers accompanying the miniature.
Collection: private collection no. 94.

John Mackintosh joined the Marines as a captain lieutenant of the 3rd company in 1793, was appointed first lieutenant in August 1805, and served aboard the *Polyphemus* at the Battle of Trafalgar. The appointment was renewed at Brighton in January 1816. He died in South Africa. His portrait by Cosway shows him as a young officer, probably painted shortly before he sailed for Trafalgar in 1805. The hair worn in queue was not fashionable after this date.

34

Richard Cosway, R.A., 1742–1821

Lady Elizabeth Bingham, c. 1799

Watercolour on ivory,
oval 73 × 58 mm ($2\frac{7}{8} \times 2\frac{1}{4}$ in),
inscribed on reverse in ink (not by the artist): *Lady Elizabeth Bingham – afterwards Vernon Harcourt – Cosway.*

HL to right, arms folded, white dress, blue sash, large hat with bows; brown eyes, long fair hair, aged about 4; sky background.
Plain gilt metal frame with love knot.

Exhibition: 'Richard and Maria Cosway', Edinburgh and London National Portrait Gallery, 1995, no. 124.
Collection: private collection no. 68.

Lady Elizabeth (1795–1838) was a daughter of Lord and Lady Richard Bingham (afterwards Earl of Lucan); in 1815 she married George Granville Harcourt, MP.

35

Richard Cosway, R.A., 1742–1821

Augustus, Duke of Sussex, c. 1791

Watercolour on ivory,
oval 81 × 67 mm (3¼ × 2⅝ in),
uninscribed.

HS to left, Windsor uniform (blue coat, red collar), star of Garter; blue eyes, powdered hair, aged 18; sky background.
Plain gilt metal frame, plaited brown hair in reverse, and a printed Dutch auction lot.

Collection: private collection no. 67.

The miniature is another version of a Cosway portrait in the Royal Collection (Walker 1992, no. 203), and is rather coarsely painted with heavy stipple modelling. The Duke was George III's sixth son.

36

Abraham Daniel, d.1806

Portrait of a Child, c.1780

Watercolour on ivory,
oval 35 × 28 mm (1⅜ × 1⅛ in),
uninscribed.

HS slightly to right, yellow dress with broad lacy collar; large blue eyes, long fair hair, startled expression, aged about 4; plain light buff background.
Gold diamanté brooch locket.

Collection: private collection no. 35.

37

Abraham Daniel, d. 1806

Lady in White, c. 1790

Watercolour on ivory,
oval 51 × 38 mm (2 × 1½ in),
uninscribed.

HS to right, low-cut white dress with puffed sleeves; large hazel eyes with white dot in pupils, mass of long powdered hair, rosebud mouth, aged 18 to 20; plain grey background.
Fine hinged locket opening to reveal elegant curls of brown hair, the borders and reverse of green and gold enamel and glass.

Collection: private collection no. 78.

38

Abraham Daniel, d. 1806

Portrait of a Child, thought to be Princess Charlotte Augusta, 1798–99

Watercolour on ivory,
oval 50 × 39 mm (2 × 1½ in),
uninscribed.

HL to right, white dress, broad blue sash, white lacy bonnet with blue bow; large hazel eyes, long fair hair, pink complexion, rosebud mouth, aged about 2; plain buff background.
Gold frame with a blue enamel and split pearl border, the reverse with blue enamel border and window revealing brown silk; red travelling case.

Collections: Edward Paine collection, sold Christie's 28 October 1980 (142); Mrs Albert Hoffman collection; private collection no. 30.

The portrait has for some time been identified with Princess Charlotte Augusta, the Prince Regent's daughter, born in 1796, married to Leopold, King of the Belgians, in 1816, and died in childbirth in 1817. In other early portraits, by Cosway and others, she has the wide mouth and brilliant blue eyes of the Hanoverians, making the authenticity of this miniature doubtful.

39

Joseph Daniel, *c.* 1760–1803

Portrait of an Officer, c. 1795

Watercolour on ivory,
oval 85 × 53 mm (3⅜ × 2⅛ in),
uninscribed.

HS to right, uniform of the London and Westminster Light Horse; grey eyes, powdered hair in queue, aged about 25; plain grey background.

Collections: Vincent family; private collection no. 95.

Joseph and Abraham Daniel, two of three brothers working as jewellers and miniaturists in Bath and Plymouth, are noted for their characteristic style of painting which includes huge melting eyes and a glossy texture due to the use of gum arabic. This picture is believed to be a member of the Vincent family. The Holburne Museum has a portrait attributed to Joseph Daniel, also of about this date and slightly tighter in style.

40

'V', fl. *c.* 1775–80

Man in a Dark Blue Coat, c. 1780

Watercolour on ivory,
oval 61 × 50 mm (2⅜ × 2 in),
uninscribed.

HS to right, dark blue coat with brass buttons, white spotted waistcoat, white shirt frill; hazel eyes, short powdered hair, large head, colourless face, aged 30 to 40; plain grey background.
Lightly chased gold locket with plaited hair.

Collection: private collection no. 79.

The miniaturist signing his work with a cursive 'V' is known from two examples, noted by Basil Long at auction in 1926 and 1928. One was of about 1778. They both had grey backgrounds, the faces shaded with grey, and the heads disproportionately large. This picture seems to fit these characteristics.

41

Thomas Day, *c.* 1732–1807

The Revd Archibald Alison, c. 1785

Watercolour on ivory,
oval 40 × 31 mm (1½ × 1¼ in),
uninscribed.

HS to left, black coat and waistcoat; blue eyes, powdered hair, face firmly modelled with bluish stipple, timid expression.
Gold frame with chased rim and plain reverse engraved: *Revd Archibald Alison.*

Collections: formerly attributed to Charles Shirreff; private collection no. 50.

The portrait is here attributed to Thomas Day, believed to have been a pupil of Ozias Humphry and an RA exhibitor 1773–88. The sitter, Archibald Alison (1757–1839), was painted by Raeburn and there is a marble bust of him in the Scottish National Portrait Gallery, but 'he seems to have led a studious, retired and rather indolent life, generally lying in bed, "reading and thinking", till two in the afternoon' (Leslie Stephen in *Dictionary of National Biography*, citing Sir Archibald Alison's *Autobiography*).

42

Philip Jean, 1755–1802

Lady in White and Violet, c. 1785

Watercolour on ivory,
oval 83 × 68 mm (3¼ × 2⅝ in),
uninscribed.

TQL to right, seated on a red sofa, white low-cut dress, the sleeves decorated with pearls, violet ribbon sash and matching ribbon in her powdered hair; large brown eyes, aged about 20; pillar, red curtain and sky background.

Collections: Charles E. Lees 1997; private collection no. 100.

43

Philip Jean, 1755–1802

Man in Blue, c. 1790

Watercolour on ivory,
oval 61 × 50 mm (2⅜ × 2 in),
uninscribed.

HS to left, dark blue coat, brass buttons, red waistcoat, white shirt frill and bow tie; hazel eyes, powdered wig, aged 50–60; sky background.
Locket with plain gold rim and copper back.

Collection: private collection no. 22.

44

Philip Jean, 1755–1802

Man in Brown, c. 1790

Watercolour on ivory,
oval 50 × 39 mm (2 × 1½ in),
uninscribed.

HS to left, brown coat with white collar and lapels, white neckcloth and shirt frill; blue eyes, powdered wig, serious expression, aged 30–40; sky background. Gold locket with blue glass borders decorated with gold leaves and flowers, plait of hair in the back.

Collection: private collection no. 37.

Philip Jean was born in the Channel Isles, served in the Royal Navy under Rodney, and began to exhibit miniatures at the Royal Academy in 1787, though an early portrait by him of a girl in a pink dress and white turban, dated 1782, is in the Royal Collection. Jean did a lot of work for George III and his family in the 1790s, and it is possible that these two elegantly dressed gentlemen were members of the Royal Household. No. 44 has a specially decorative locket. No. 42, an unusually large miniature, may be compared to the striking 1788 portrait of the marine artist, Dominic Serres, in the National Portrait Gallery (Fig. 20 on p. 41).

16

45

George Engleheart, 1750–1829

Lady in Blue, 1780–85

Watercolour on ivory,
oval 50 × 43 mm (2 × 1⅝ in) sight size,
uninscribed.

HS profile to right, blue dress trimmed with fur, pink cloak, blue hair ribbon, double pearl necklace, red and blue bow at her bosom; grey eyes, brown upswept hair; plain background, darker to right.
Plain gold locket with pearl border.

Exhibition: 'La Peinture Anglaise', Louvre, 1938, lent by T. Hugh Cobb.
Collections: T. Hugh Cobb; private collection no. 13.

46

George Engleheart, 1750–1829

Girl in a Black Hat, c.1785

Watercolour on ivory,
oval 57 × 48 mm (2¼ × 1⅞ in),
uninscribed.

HL to left, facing, white frilly dress, blue sash, large black hat with plumes; huge brown eyes, pale rather podgy face modelled with grey strokes, fringe of fair curly hair to shoulders, aged 7 or 8; sky background.
Locket set with a large paste diamond, fair hair in the back tied with a love-knot within a blue and gold enamel border.

Collection: private collection no. 14.

George Engleheart is considered, without doubt, one of the most distinguished miniaturists of all time, and specially of this period. He was immensely productive, and his skill and industry appealed to George III who had the good sense to appoint him Miniature Painter to the King in 1789. These two miniatures (nos. 45 and 46) are characteristic of his middle period, painted on small ivories, especially the girl whose enormous eyes and dashing hat are hallmarks of his work at this time. The Collection is rich in Engleheart miniatures, and examples of his later phases are on pp. 178–83.

47

George Engleheart, 1750–1829

Young Lady in White, c. 1785

Watercolour on ivory,
oval 43 × 34 mm (1⅝ × 1⅜ in),
uninscribed.

HS to right, white frilly dress with bow at the bosom; large dark wide open eyes, long brownish hair with pearls, serious face with strong nose shadow, aged 18 to 19; sky background.
Hinged gold locket with dark brown plait of hair.

Collection: private collection no. 15.

48

George Engleheart, 1750–1829

Young Lady in White, c. 1785

Watercolour on ivory,
oval 43 × 34 mm (1⅝ × 1⅜ in),
uninscribed.

HS to left, white frilly dress, pearl necklace; large dark brown eyes, long nose, long dark brown hair with white ribbon, severe expression, aged 20–25; sky background.
Hinged gold locket with light brown plait of hair.

Collection: private collection no. 16.

The two portraits are hinged together and probably are of two sisters though there does not seem to be any strong family likeness.

49

George Engleheart, 1750–1829

Lady in Black, c. 1785

Watercolour on ivory,
oval 51 × 40 mm (2 × 1½ in),
uninscribed.

HS to right, black dress over a white chemise with spreading collar, black hat with a white plume; blue eyes, curled powdered hair, aged 40 to 50; sky background. Plain gold locket.

Collection: private collection no. 17.

50

George Engleheart, 1750–1829

Lady in White, 1785–90

Watercolour on ivory,
oval 53 × 39 mm (2⅛ × 1½ in),
uninscribed.

HS, head turned to right, white dress with frilled border and turquoise bow at her bosom; dark blue eyes, curled and powdered hair with blue and white ribbons, pale face, long nose, aged about 30; sky background. Chased gold locket with plait of dark brown hair, in its original leather box.

Collection: private collection no. 18.

51

George Engleheart, 1750–1829

Lord Mountjoy, c. 1784

Watercolour on ivory,
oval 49 × 38 mm (2 × 1½ in) sight size,
uninscribed.

HS to right, blue coat with upstanding collar and brass buttons, white shirt frill and bow tie; large blue eyes, powdered wig, aged 25–30; sky background. Original hinged double locket with plaited hair opposite the image; starred blue glass back and front, plaited hair in pearl oval.

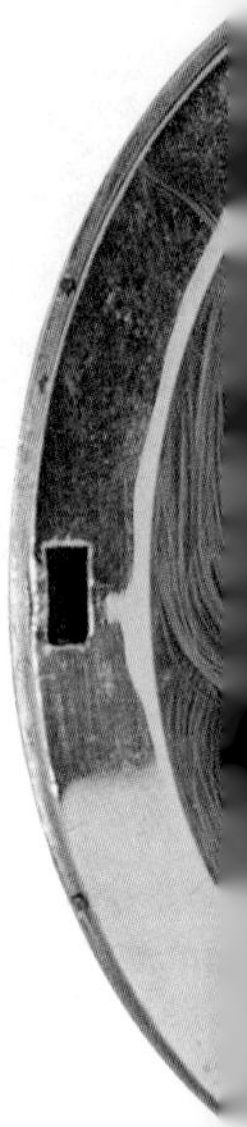

Luke Gardiner (1745–98) was MP for County Dublin, an Irish Privy Councillor, Colonel of the Dublin Militia and created Baron Mountjoy of Mountjoy, County Tyrone, in 1789. He was advanced to become a Viscount in 1795 and was killed at the head of his regiment during the Irish Revolution. His portrait was painted by Francis Cotes and Reynolds, and he commissioned the famous painting by Reynolds, *Three Ladies Adorning a Term of Hymen*, now in the Tate Gallery; he was engaged at the time to one of the ladies, Elizabeth Montgomery, whom he married in 1773, but she died in childbed in the same year. Engleheart's portrait appears in the Fee Book under the year 1784 as 'Mr Gardiner'.

Collections: Lady Currie (British Embassy Rome 1902); private collection no. 20.

52

George Engleheart, 1750–1829

Catherine Inglis, 1790

Watercolour on ivory,
oval 45 × 35 mm (1¾ × 1⅜ in),
uninscribed.

HS to right, frilly white dress with blue ribbons; dark brown eyes, matching ribbon in her long curled powdered hair, aged 25–30; grey background darker to left. Plain gold locket, oval window in back with plait, the sides engraved: *Catherine Inglis Painted 1790 in her 31 Year.*

Literature: Engleheart's Fee Book, '1790 Mrs Inglis'.
Collections: Sotheby's 28 July 1980 (270); private collection no. 39.

53

George Engleheart, 1750–1829

Mrs Samuel Stephens, 1790

Watercolour on ivory,
oval 73 × 58 mm (2⅞ × 2¼ in),
uninscribed.

HL to right, flounced white dress, arms slashed to reveal yellow lining, turquoise sash; large brown eyes, long curled powdered hair with white ribbon and cap, smiling, aged 20–25; sky background.
Plain gilt easel locket engraved: *Mrs Samuel Stephens By G. Engleheart 1790.*

Literature: Engleheart's Fee Book, '1792 Mr Stephens; 1800 Mrs and Mr Stephens'.
Collections: S.J. Phillips (advertisement in *Burlington Magazine*, October 1934); private collection no. 40.

54

George Engleheart, 1750–1829

Miss Channing, 1805–10

Watercolour on ivory,
oval 75 × 62 mm (3 × 2½ in),
possibly signed indistinctly, lower left, with cursive *E*.

HL to right, high-waisted white dress; large grey eyes, short dark brown hair, aged 25–30; sky background.
Plain brass frame with claws on red velvet backing.

Exhibition: Engleheart Exhibition, Victoria and Albert Museum, 1929, no. 149 (as 'Miss Canning'), lent by Miss Grant Robertson.
Collection: private collection no. 41.

George Engleheart's Fee Book records a payment for Miss Channing in the year 1785, but this portrait must be much later. The clothes, hair style, and larger ivory suggest a date of about 1805–10.

55

Jean-Louis Voille, 1744–*c.* 1802

The Empress Maria Feodorovna and six of her children, 1788

Watercolour on oval ivories, framed in gold lockets mounted on blue glass in a large oval gold frame engraved: *Fait au moi de Septembre de l'année 1788.*

1. In the centre is Maria Feodorovna (1759–1828), née Princess Sophia Dorothea of Württemberg; she married in 1776 Tsar Paul I, son of Peter III and Catherine the Great.
2. Alexander (1777–1825), later succeeded his father as Tsar Alexander I.
3. Constantine (1779–1831), married (1) in 1796, Juliana of Saxe-Coburg-Saalfeld, and (2) in 1820, Joanna of Grudna-Grudzinscy.
4. Alexandra (1783–1801), married in 1799, the Archduke Joseph of Austria.
5. Helena (1784–1803), married in 1799, Frederick of Mecklenburg-Schwerin, a nephew of Queen Charlotte of Great Britain.
6. Marie (1786–1859), married in 1804, Grand Duke Charles Frederick of Saxe-Weimar-Eisenbach.
7. Catherine (1788–1819), married (1) in 1809, George Duke of Oldenburg, and (2) in 1816, William I, King of Württemberg.

They had four more children, including Nicholas (1796–1855) who succeeded his brother Alexander, in 1825, as Tsar Nicholas I.

Exhibition: 'Anna Pavlova and the Russian Court', Palace Het Loo, Apeldoorn, Holland, October 1995.
Collections: the group of miniatures, probably by Voille, was given by Paul I as a birthday present to Maria Feodorovna, 20 September 1788. It was in the Hermitage Collection, St Petersburg, until the dispersal after the Revolution. Private collection no. 65.

Voille was a Parisian artist who worked for some time at the Russian Courts in Moscow and St Petersburg.

56

John Bogle, 1746–1803

General Prescott, 1789

Watercolour on ivory,
oval 34 × 28 mm (1⅜ × 1⅛ in),
signed and dated lower right: *IB / 1789.*

HS to right in general officer's uniform; light brown eyes, short powdered wig in queue, aged 50; plain buff background.
Gold bracelet locket engraved: *General Prescott Gov. of Canada. By J. Bogle 1789.*

Collection: private collection no. 28.

John Bogle was born in Edinburgh. He worked as a miniaturist there and in London where this portrait of Prescott was doubtless painted. It is a copy of an earlier miniature (now in the National Portrait Gallery) painted in 1776 when the General had returned home on leave after the storming of Fort Washington. It shows the neat stipple modelling characteristic of Bogle's rather diffident style. Robert Prescott joined the army in 1755, served with General Wolfe in North America, and was appointed Governor General of Canada in 1797.

57

Horace Hone, 1754–1825

Man in a Dark Grey Coat, c. 1790

Watercolour on ivory,
oval 78 × 62 mm (3 × 2½ in),
uninscribed.

HS to left, dark grey coat, white neckcloth and bow tie; grey eyes, powdered wig in queue, podgy pale face rather coarsely painted, beaky nose, aged *c.* 40; stormy sky background.

Oval brass rim frame with claw fastening, in a plain ebonised wood rectangle. On the back is a paper seal with a coat of arms in laurel wreaths, and the number 70.

Collection: private collection no. 8.

58

Horace Hone (attributed to)

Man in a Fur Collar, c. 1795

Plumbago on card,
oval 81 × 63 mm (3¼ × 2½ in) sight size,
uninscribed.

HS nearly profile to right, coat with fur collar; pointed nose, wide mouth, aged *c.* 25; plain grey background.
Dark brown moulded wood frame.

Collection: private collection no. 49.

Horace Hone, a son of the Irish painter Nathaniel Hone, was born in London, attended the Royal Academy Schools and exhibited miniatures there for fifty years. He usually signed his works with a monogram HH, and they are often painted with the rich colouring of oils. This plumbago drawing is an interesting addition to the Hone corpus. A completed miniature of the same subject (85 mm, wearing a buff-coloured coat with brown fur collar), also attributed to Horace Hone, was sold by Phillips, 8 July 1997 (219).

59

Andrew Plimer, 1763–1837

Lady in White Dress and Blue Sash, 1785–90

Watercolour on ivory,
oval 94 × 72 mm (3⅝ × 2⅞ in),
uninscribed.

HL to left, white dress, narrow blue belt; brown eyes, huge powdered wig, smiling expression, aged about 20; sky background.
Gold locket with blue glass reverse enclosing a lock of brown hair tied with a gold love-knot.

Collection: private collection no. 6.

60

Andrew Plimer, 1763–1837

Lady in White Wearing a Miniature, 1785–90

Watercolour on ivory,
oval 78 × 63 mm (3 × 2½ in),
uninscribed.

HL to left, white dress, pearl necklace with a miniature of a man in red, in profile to left; brown eyes, luxuriant powdered hair tied with a white bandeau, aged about 20; sky background.
Gold locket with dark blue glass reverse enclosing two plumes of fair and brown hair tied, in the shape of a sheaf of corn, with a seed pearl ring.

Collection: private collection no. 7.

61

Michael Kean, 1761–1823

John Hayes St Leger, c. 1785

Watercolour on ivory,
oval 40 × 33 mm (1½ × 1¼ in),
inscribed on reverse: *Colonel St Leger.*

HS to left, scarlet coat, yellow and white striped waistcoat, white cravat; hazel eyes, full powdered wig, aged about 30; sky background.
Plain gilt metal locket.

Exhibition: South Kensington Museum, 1865 (2589), lent by G.T. Manning.
Literature: Franklin Barrett and Arthur Thorpe, *Derby Porcelain*, 1971, pp. 61, 94–5; Gerald Pendred, 'Michael Kean and the Duesbury Miniatures', *Derby Porcelain International Society Journal 3*, 1996, p. 13.
Collections: G.T. Manning; private collection no. 32.

The sitter is almost certainly John St Leger (1756–1800), a nephew of Barry, the founder of the St Leger stake. He was a close friend and boon companion of the Prince of Wales, who appointed him Groom of the Royal Chamber. His portrait by Gainsborough, a full-length in uniform, is in the Royal Collection and the companion piece of the Prince is at Waddesdon Manor. The Prince described St Leger as 'one of ye best fellows yt. ever lived'.

Kean entered the Royal Academy Schools in 1784, exhibited miniatures there 1786–90, then joined William Duesbury at the Derby porcelain firm, became virtually director and married Duesbury's widow – an unsuccessful union ending in a bitter lawsuit.

[153]

62

Louis-Marie Sicardi, 1746–1825

Lady in White, 1790

Watercolour on ivory,
circle 59 mm (2⅜ in) diameter,
signed and dated lower right: *Sicardi 1790.*

HL to right, off-white dress, blue sash, grey shawl, spray of flowers at the bosom; blue eyes, powdered hair, aged about 20; bluish-grey background.
Gilt metal frame with white enamelled pellet borders and cream silk backing.

Collection: private collection no. 54.

The identity of the lady is unknown at present but Sicardi, who was generously employed at the court of Louis XVI, during the Revolution, under Napoleon, and by the Bourbons after the Restoration, had no difficulty in finding sitters among the rich and the good.

63

Pierre Rouvier, b. after 1742, fl. 1770–1800

Lady in Grey, c. 1790

Watercolour on ivory,
circle 57 mm (2¼ in) diameter,
uninscribed.

HS to left seated in a blue and gold chair, head turned facing, grey dress, transparent white shawl; brown eyes, long powdered hair, aged 40–45; blue curtain to left, plain grey background.
Chased gold case with green back and votive altar with motto: *je brule et ne consume jamais.*

Collection: private collection no. 99.

Rouvier was born in Aix and became a pupil at the Paris Academy in 1770. Leo Schidlof compares his work to that of Sicardi and Campana.

JE BRULE ET NE CONSUME JAMAIS

64

Richard Crosse, 1742–1810

Man in Green, c. 1790

Watercolour on ivory,
oval 53 × 44 mm (2⅛ × 1¾ in),
uninscribed.

HL to left, bottle green coat, white shirt frill; grey eyes, powdered hair, slight smile, aged about 40; sky background.
Chased gold locket with blue glass back enclosing dark brown hair tied with gold love-knot on a white ground.

Collection: private collection no. 90.

Richard Crosse was born in Devonshire, a deaf mute, but prospered in London and exhibited miniatures there from 1760 to 1796. He was appointed enamel painter to George III in 1788. He often used a bluish-green shading, giving his sitters a strange bruised appearance. His sitter-book has been published in the *Walpole Society Journal*, vol. XVII (1929).

65

Henry Jacob Burch, 1763–after 1834

Lady in White, 1791

Watercolour on ivory,
oval 66 × 56 mm (2⅝ × 2¼ in),
inscribed clearly in ink on the backing paper, *H Burch Pinxit 1791.*

HS to left, white dress with high white collar, pearl necklace with a Wedgwood profile of a man; blue eyes, long straight nose, powdered hair, self-confident expression, aged 25 to 30; sky background.
Plain gold frame with narrow rim and window in back revealing the inscription.

Collection: private collection no. 45.

Henry Burch entered the Royal Academy Schools in 1779 and exhibited, not only miniatures, there and elsewhere in London between 1787 and 1834. The lady here has been identified with Mrs Fitzherbert but this cannot be sustained; Mrs Fitzherbert, beloved of the Prince Regent and painted many times by Gainsborough, Reynolds, Romney and specially Cosway, was famous for her beauty and her 'melting brown eyes' (see catalogue no. 31).

66

Charles Shirreff, ***c.*** **1750–after 1831**

Miss Lydia White, 1794

Watercolour on ivory,
oval 58 × 45 mm (2¼ × 1¾ in),
uninscribed.

HL to right, white dress, blue sash, white head-scarf; hazel eyes, long powdered hair, pale face, head tilted backwards.
Plain gold locket with blue glass reverse with brown hair and the monogram *JD* in a pearl lozenge.

Collection: private collection no. 19.

Charles Shirreff came from Edinburgh and entered the Royal Academy Schools in 1769. He was deaf and dumb and, perhaps for this reason, concentrated on theatrical scenes and portraits where facial expressions could easily be seen. He worked in Bath, India and London. Criss-cross hatching in the modelling and backgrounds is a feature of his style.

67

François Ferrière, 1752–1839 (attributed to)

Man with long powdered hair, c. 1795

Watercolour on ivory,
oval 77 × 60 mm (3 × 2⅜ in),
uninscribed.

HS to left, dark grey coat, white collar and cravat; light brown eyes, pale face modelled to imitate oil painting, long untidy powdered hair in queue; black background.
Plain gold locket.

Collection: private collection no. 4.

Ferrière was born in Geneva but worked mainly in Paris, London and St Petersburg. He exhibited miniatures in London in 1793–1804 and 1817–22, hallmarks of his work being the Swiss style of stipple modelling and opaque backgrounds. The identity of the sitter is unknown at present but, if he was painted in London, his rebellious aspect suggests a Foxite sympathiser.

68

Henry Edridge, 1768–1821

Man in Red, c. 1795

Watercolour on ivory,
oval 85 × 67 mm (3⅜ × 2⅝ in),
uninscribed.

HL to left, red velvet coat with large falling collar, lace shirt frill; blue eyes, powdered hair, aged 25 to 30; sky background and corn stooks.
Plain gilt metal frame with plait of light brown hair.

Collection: private collection no. 57.

69

Henry Edridge, 1768–1821

Marmaduke Sealy, c. 1800

Watercolour on card,
oval 76 × 64 mm (3 × 2½ in),
uninscribed.

HS to left, black coat, white shirt and cravat; dark eyes, untidy grey hair, aged about 40; foliage and sky background.
Gold frame engraved: *Marmaduke Sealy* and with the diamond initial *S* surrounded by plaited hair on blue glass.

Collection: private collection no. 96.

Henry Edridge exhibited at the Royal Academy from 1786 to his death in 1821. His miniatures are often marked by heavy shadows under the eyes (not in these two) and by a sharp shadow under the nose. He was taken up by Queen Charlotte at Windsor Castle where, in 1802, he made small whole-length watercolour drawings of the Royal Family. There is an interesting group of Edridge miniatures, of the Hoare family, at Stourhead, Wiltshire.

70

Sir William Beechey (after)

Princess Amelia, c. 1797

Watercolour on ivory,
oval 80 × 63 mm ($3\frac{1}{8}$ × $2\frac{1}{2}$ in),
uninscribed.

HL to left, head turned to right, pale blue dress, dark blue sash, white turban hat, gold chain necklace; blue eyes, powdered hair; brownish-red curtain background. Plain gold locket.

Literature: Walker 1992, pp. 171–2, no. 346.
Collections: bought from the Anglesey family; private collection no. 69.

The portrait is one of many copies of a miniature in the Royal Collection tentatively attributed to Ann Phyllis, Lady Beechey. This in turn derives from Sir William Beechey's oil also in the Royal Collection and painted for the Prince of Wales in about 1797. It was engraved for *La Belle Assemblée* in 1806 and lettered 'from an original miniature in the possession of H.R.H. Princess Elizabeth', without mention of the artist's name. Princess Amelia was George III and Queen Charlotte's youngest child.

[169]

71

Mathias Finucane, fl. *c.* 1798 (attributed to)

Royal Artillery Officer, c. 1798

Watercolour on ivory,
oval 70 × 53 mm ($2\frac{3}{4} \times 2\frac{1}{8}$ in),
uninscribed but possibly signed on reverse.

HL to right, dark blue military uniform, scarlet and gold collar and facings, gold epaulettes with one white star; grey eyes, pale face with waxy blue-grey modelling, white hair, aged about 50; cloudy sky background.
Plain gold locket with plait of brown hair in small oval 'window'.

Collection: private collection no. 60.

Miniatures by Finucane, possibly from Guernsey, are scarce. His characteristics seem to have been modelling by colour and brown outlines, and a general pallor.

72

Archibald Skirving, 1749–1819

Man in Dark Blue, 1798

Watercolour on ivory,
oval 67 × 56 mm (2⅝ × 2¼ in),
signed and dated lower left: *AS / 1798*.

HS to left, dark blue coat, white waistcoat, white neckcloth and cravat; hazel eyes, short brown hair, solid face strongly modelled with broad strokes, aged about 50; cloudy sky background.
Plain gold locket.

Literature: Foskett 1987, p. 646.
Exhibition: 'Raeburn's Rival', Scottish National Portrait Gallery, Edinburgh, 1999 (122).
Collections: Grossmann; Edward Paine collection; private collection no. 87.

Archibald Skirving was one of the outstanding Scottish portrait painters, working in miniature, oil and specially coloured chalk. He has been described as easily bearing comparison with Ramsay and Raeburn, and as a pastellist can be classed with the great eighteenth-century artists alongside Rosalba, Liotard, John Russell and Hugh Douglas Hamilton. This miniature, one of only a few he signed and dated, is possibly one of the last he painted; his eyesight had been damaged when a prisoner in France and on his return to Edinburgh he turned more and more to pastel work, a less exacting medium in which he undoubtedly excelled.

73

William Wood, 1769–1810

Sir William Beaumarris Rush, 1798

Watercolour on ivory,
oval 96 × 79 mm (3¾ × 3⅛ in),
signed and dated on reverse: *Sir Wm Beaumaurice Rush / Born Sept 1st 1750 / by Willm Wood / Cork St. London.*

HL to right, blue coat, white waistcoat and shirt frill; grey eyes, powdered hair, aged about 50; cloudy sky background. Chased gilt metal case with claw back.

Collection: private collection no. 72.

74

William Wood, 1769–1810

Lady Rush, 1796

Watercolour on ivory,
oval 96 × 79 mm (3¾ × 3⅛ in),
uninscribed.

HL to left, head looking to right, high-waisted white dress with gold cord; brown eyes, long powdered hair with three white ribbons, lips slightly open, aged 40 to 50; cloudy sky background.
Chased gilt metal case with claw back on rectangular black lacquer frame.

Literature: Wood Memorandum, nos. 5624, 5445.
Collection: private collection no. 73.

Wood entered the Royal Academy Schools in 1785 and exhibited miniatures in London 1788–1808. He used short brush strokes and warm colouring, and his men sometimes have brick-red faces. His sitter books are an invaluable source of information, with size and colour notes and other interesting details. No. 71 is listed as: *5624 Mr William Rush of Pall Mall. 3rd size July Find 13 Nov 1798 Decr 23rd About 48 – 62*

[continued at foot of p. 176]

75

George Engleheart, 1750–1829

Lady in White, 1795–1800

Watercolour on ivory,
oval 72 × 58 mm (2⅞ × 2¼ in) sight size,
labelled on reverse: *Engleheart pinxit.*

HL facing, white dress (unfinished), blue sash, white frilly hat with feather; large blue eyes, powdered hair falling down back, slight smile; sky background. Plain gilt metal frame with claw back under red leather.

Exhibition: label on reverse, 'George Engleheart', Victoria and Albert Museum, 1929 (288), lent by Lt-Col. E.L. Engleheart, though no. 288 was a portrait of the Rev. Henry Engleheart by the nephew JCDE. At least twelve 'Lady' miniatures were lent to this exhibition by the Lieutenant-Colonel.
Collection: private collection no. 12.

No. 74: *continued from previous page*

red – coat of 6 – Hume's white: 120 – sun burnt but fair Complex. = 104 – Breath'd on – some red chalk – Light varied background – gum touches – Powdered hair. Another version, listed as 5973 and with a small tracing in red ink, was begun in February 1803 and finished in June. No. 74 is listed as: *5445 Mrs Rush of Wimbledon: in a white dress & open turban – averted dark eye – Gold cord round waist – silver behind head – Cr⁰ in girdle – 8th size about 35. M's white Fin^d 14 Sep 1796 Decr 15th.*

William Rush was knighted 19 June 1800.

76

George Engleheart, 1750–1829

Young Man in Blue, c. 1800

Watercolour on ivory,
oval 80 × 67 mm (3 1/8 × 2 5/8 in),
signed with cursive *E.*

HL to right, dark blue coat with brass buttons, white neckcloth and cravat; large dark eyes, fair hair over forehead, curvey lips, aged 20 to 25; sky background. Plain gold locket with dark brown hair in back and gold monogram TAC or TAP.

Literature: Reynolds 1988, pp. 141–2.
Collection: private collection no. 38.

77

George Engleheart, 1750–1829

Lady in White, c. 1800

Watercolour on ivory,
oval 80 × 63 mm (3⅛ × 2½ in),
dated on reverse: *Feb. 14th.*

HL to right, white dress, sash, shoulder frills, bow tie; large blue eyes, long curled powdered hair, white cap, aged about 50; sky background.
Plain gold frame with loop.

Collection: private collection no. 53.

Engleheart's early miniatures were usually painted on small ivories and latterly, between 1780 and 1791, the ladies and girls often wore the fashionable large 'Gainsborough' hats at a rakish angle, as in No. 46 (see page 128). Later the size of the ivories increased, the clothes became less flamboyant, the men dressed in black or grey, and the women were treated as human beings with no flinching from their physical shortcomings. As Graham Reynolds has perceptively remarked, England was changing and Engleheart's customers had turned from the aristocracy to the shopkeeper.

78

George Engleheart, 1750–1829

Sir Charles Flint, c. 1802 ?Captain G. Flint

Watercolour on ivory,
oval 81 × 63 mm (3¼ × 2½ in),
signed with cursive *E.*

HS to right, dark blue coat with brass buttons, white waistcoat, shirt frill and bow tie; blue eyes, short grey (powdered) hair, smug expression, aged about 50; cloudy sky background.
Gilt and chased metal frame with clawed back.

Literature: Engleheart's Fee Book, '1802 Mr Flint, 1808 Captain G. Flint'.
Collections: label on back inscribed: *Anna Letitia Flint given by her Father GWF;* private collection no. 25.

79

George Engleheart, 1750–1829

Anna Maria Flint, 1802

Watercolour on ivory,
oval 79 × 63 mm (3⅛ × 2½ in),
signed with cursive *E.*

HS to right, white dress with ruffed collar and yellow sash; dark eyes, black hair piled up and tied with black ribbon, plump face, aged 25 to 30; sky background.
Plain brass rim with clawed back.

Literature: Engleheart's Fee Book, '1802 Mr Flint, 1808 Mrs Flint'.
Collections: probably G.W. Flint and his daughter as above; private collection no. 26.

80

John Smart, 1742/3–1811

Rear-Admiral Robert Williams, 1801

Watercolour on ivory,
oval 79 × 63 mm (3⅛ × 2½ in),
signed and dated lower left: *JS / 1801*.

HS to left, dark blue coat with black velvet collar and brass buttons, white waistcoat, shirt and neckcloth; brown eyes, curly white hair, pale podgy face, aged 36; cloudy sky background.
Gold case engraved: *Robert Williams*, with plaited hair and initials *RW* on opalescent glass.

Literature: Foskett 1964, pp. 59, 76.
Collections: family descent; private collection no. 97.

81

John Smart, 1742/3–1811

Ivy Williams, 1801

Watercolour on ivory,
oval 79 × 63 mm (3⅛ × 2½ in),
signed and dated lower left: *JS / 1801*.

HS to right, white high-waisted dress with ruffled collar and tied sash; brown eyes, brown hair tied with brown ribbon and pearls, aged about 25; cloudy sky background.
Gold case to match No. 80, engraved: *Ivy Williams*, with plaited hair and initials *EIW*.

Literature: Foskett 1964, pp. 59, 76.
Collections: family descent; private collection no. 98.

Smart's habit of allowing the ivory to show through the watercolour gives a characteristic translucence to the faces and neck in both these beautiful examples of his

[continued at foot of p. 186]

82

Franz Gerhard von Kügelgen, 1772–1820

Empress Maria Feodorovna, c. 1801

Watercolour on ivory,
oval 71 × 58 mm (2¾ × 2¼ in),
signed top right: *Kügelgen.*

HS to right, black dress, black veil, a miniature of Paul I on a chain, and an Order; blue eyes, light brown hair under widow's veil.
Octagonal gold and tortoiseshell frame in a red leather travelling case with brass tablets engraved in Russian, above: *This book of the Emperor Alexander I was presented by the Emperor Nicholas I to D.T.C. Prince Nicho. Galitzin,* and below: *A Portrait of Empress Maria presented by Her Majesty to him also.*

Collections: Galitzin family; Charles Woollett & Son, 1966 (reproduced in *Connoisseur*, August 1966); private collection no. 29.

No. 81: *continued from previous page*

later work. For earlier Smart miniatures see Nos. 23–6. Robert Williams's naval career is recorded in John Marshall's *Naval Biography*, 1823, pp. 856–61. He was first lieutenant of the *Prince George* at the Battle of Cape St Vincent, put on half-pay in 1798, a flag-captain at the time of this miniature, and appointed rear-admiral in 1823. He died at home, in Queen's Square, Bath, in 1827, his wife Ivy having predeceased him by two years in 1825. Her portrait by Smart was copied by Edward Nash in India in 1802.

Сiя книжка Императора Алек-
сандра I го пожалована Импера-
торомъ Николаемъ I мъ Д. Т. С. Кн.
Алекс. Ник. Голицыну.
Портретъ Императрицы Марiи
пожалованъ Ея Величе=
ствомъ ему же.

83

Franz Gerhard von Kügelgen, 1772–1820

Theresa von Thurn und Taxis, c. 1789

Watercolour on ivory,
oval 66 × 54 mm (2⅝ × 2⅛ in),
uninscribed on obverse. but on backing card in ink: *Therese Gemählin des Fürsten Karl Alexander v. Thurn u Taxis, Tochter des Herzogs Karls II von Mecklenburg-Strelitz, Schwester der Königin Luise, geb. d. 5 April 1773 vermählt d. 25 Mai 1789 + 12 Febr 1839 K61.*

HL to right, head to left, white dress, gold corsage with equestrian border, magnificent polychrome turban; hazel eyes, dark brown hair, aged about 25; lurid sky background.
Plain gilt metal locket.

Collection: private collection no. 56.

Von Kügelgen was born in Bacharach in 1772, studied for some years in Italy, then went to Russia where he was appointed Court painter and a member of the Academy of St Petersburg. He was murdered near Dresden, 27 March 1820. His works are scarce but, judging from these two signed miniatures, of outstanding quality.

Therese
Gema des Fürsten Karl
Alexander v. Thurn u. Taxis
Tochter des Herzogs Karl II.
von Mecklenburg-Strelitz,
Schwester der Königin Luise,
geb. d. 5. April 1773
vermählt d. 25. Mai 1789
† d. 12. Febr. 1839.
3
K. 61.

84

Richard Collins, 1755–1831

General Champneys, c. 1805

Watercolour on ivory,
oval 81 × 68 mm (3¼ × 2⅝ in),
uninscribed.

HS to right in uniform (scarlet with blue facings and collar), black neckcloth; blue eyes, fair grizzled hair, supercilious expression, aged about 45; mottled green and brown background.
Plain brass case engraved: *General Champneys / Collins.*

Collections: Anglesey family; private collection no. 70.

The sitter is probably William Champneys, who joined the army as an ensign in 1768, was appointed lieutenant in 1770 and captain in 1780, and transferred to the East India Company administration service in 1784, working in Madras. As far as is known Collins never went to India, as many other English miniaturists did, so the portrait was doubtless painted when the General returned on leave or retired.

85

Thomas Hargreaves, 1774–1846/7

Lady in a White Bonnet, 1807

Watercolour on ivory,
oval 89 × 74 mm (3½ × 2⅞ in),
signed and dated along right edge: *Hargreaves 1807,* and on backing paper in ink:
Octr 1807. T. Hargreaves pinx^{t}., and faintly in pencil: LEIGH.

HL to left in white low-cut dress, lace bonnet tied under chin; brown eyes, large nose, dark hair, rueful expression; cloudy sky background.
Machined brass rim with clawed back in standard ebonised frame with bunch of grapes hanger.

Collection: private collection no. 1.

86

Thomas Hargreaves, 1774–1846/7

Lady with Coral Necklace, c. 1808

Watercolour on ivory,
oval 82 × 69 mm (3¼ × 2¾ in),
signed and dated on backing card in ink: *Hargreaves / March 180?* (last figure indistinct – perhaps 8).

HL to left, white dress, pink shawl, coral necklace; dark brown eyes, black hair, yellowish light under cheek and chin, pert expression, aged about 18.
Plain brass rim with clawed back over red leather in standard ebonised frame with foliage hanger.

Collections: Leigh collection; private collection no. 2.

Hargreaves was born in Liverpool, was apprenticed to Lawrence, and exhibited in Liverpool and London between 1798 and 1835. His self-portrait is in the Walker Art Gallery, Liverpool, and an interesting group of Williams family miniatures by Hargreaves is at Charlecote Park. A large collection of his preliminary drawings for miniatures is in the City of Liverpool library, which might possibly lead to the identification of Nos. 85–8, perhaps of the Leigh family.

87

Thomas Hargreaves, 1774–1846/7

Young Man in Blue, 1808

Watercolour on ivory,
oval 91 × 75 mm (3½ × 3 in),
signed and dated on backing paper in ink: *Hargreaves Jany 1808,* and faintly in pencil *Leigh.*

HL to right, dark blue coat, cream waistcoat, white shirt and bow tie; brown eyes, black hair, aged 20 to 25; plain buff background.
Framed as No. 85.

Collections: Leigh collection; private collection no. 3.

88

Thomas Hargreaves, 1774–1846/7

Lady in White, 1812

Watercolour on ivory,
oval 80 × 65 mm (3⅛ × 2½ in),
inscribed on backing paper: *Hargreaves pinx^t. 1812.*

HL to right, high-waisted white dress, brown shawl; hazel eyes, short curly black hair, rosy complexion; trees and stormy sky background.
Plain gold locket with plaited hair and gold monogram *MB*.

Collections: Leigh collection; private collection no. 33.

89

Louis-Antoine Collas, *c.*1775–after 1833

Pauline, Queen of Württemberg, c. 1810

Watercolour on ivory,
oval 72 × 60 mm (2⅞ × 2⅜ in),
uninscribed in front but in pencil on backing card: *Königin Pauline von Württemberg.*

HL to left, head to front, low-cut transparent dress, green shawl; brown eyes, close-fitting curly brown hair, round face, aged 18–20; plain grey background. Plain gilt metal locket with small claws.

Collection: private collection no. 55.

Collas was born in Bordeaux, exhibited at the Paris Salon 1798–1816, and lived in St Petersburg 1803–11 when he painted portraits of the Tsar's family. Pauline, daughter of Duke Ludwig of Württemberg, married her brother-in-law, Frederick I, King of Württemberg, in 1820. Collas worked in the U.S. from 1816 (New York, Charleston, Baltimore, New Orleans) and returned to France in 1829.

90

Jean-Baptiste Isabey, 1767–1855

Napoleon, 1811

Watercolour on ivory,
oval 51 × 37 mm (2 × 1½ in),
signed and dated: *Isabey 1811.*

HS to right, uniform of National Guard (dark blue, red collar and braid), riband and star of Legion of Honour; blue eyes, brown hair; sky background.
Oval case within a rectangular ormolu frame with floral decoration in spandrels and green velvet back.

Collections: Edward Grosvenor Paine collection; private collection no. 76.

Isabey was introduced to Napoleon by Hortense de Beauharnais and painted many portraits at the Imperial Court. Similar miniatures, by both Augustin and Isabey, are in the Wallace Collection. Official royal patronage continued under Louis XVIII, Charles X and Louis-Philippe.

Isabey 1811

91

N. Freese, fl.1794–1814

Lady in White, c. 1810

Watercolour on ivory,
oval 70 × 58 mm (2¾ × 2¼ in),
uninscribed.

HS to left, low-cut white Empire dress; blue eyes, light brown hair brushed up at the back and fastened with a jewelled slide, long neck, head turned facing, long face, aged 20 to 25; greenish-blue background, darker behind her body.
Plain gilt metal locket.

Collection: private collection no. 58.

N. (probably Nathaniel) Freese exhibited miniatures in London between 1794 and 1814. Examples of his work are in the Fitzwilliam Museum, at Ickworth and Polesden Lacey, and a specially attractive one, also of a lady in a white dress and of about the same date as the miniature shown here, in the Holburne Museum (M123). The background darker to one side seems to be a characteristic of his miniatures.

92

George Chinnery, 1774–1852

Marian Greer, c. 1810

Watercolour on ivory,
oval 85 × 70 mm (3⅜ × 2¾ in),
uninscribed.

HL to left, back view, head nearly in profile, white dress with broad white collar, pearl necklace; dark eyes, dark brown hair tied with a white scarf under her chin, strong features, commanding expression, aged 25 to 30; brown background darker to right.

Rectangular ormolu frame mounted on black lacquered wood with acorn hanger, on the back a paper inscribed: *Harriet / Portrait of Marian Greer, cousin and 1st wife of Sir Charles D'Oyly (known as the 'famous amateur painter'). He was a brother of my grandmother, Harriet Rochford D'Oyly who married George Baring.*

Literature: Conner 1993, pp. 89, 93.
Collection: private collection no. 77.

Chinnery entered the Royal Academy Schools in 1792 and exhibited there till 1846. From 1802 he worked in India where he is believed to have taught painting to Marian's husband, Sir Charles D'Oyly, an official at the Calcutta Court of Appeal. A pair of miniatures of them both, in a similar pose and also by Chinnery, was sold at Christie's, 7 November 1988 (92).

93

Alfred Edward Chalon, 1780–1860

Elizabeth Bone, c. 1815

Watercolour on card,
rectangle 87 × 66 mm (3½ × 2⅝ in),
signed top left in white paint: *A Chalon*, and inscribed on the backing paper:
Elizabeth Deborah Bone / Born Jan^{ry} 30. 1795 / Died June 3 1855 / Buried at Brompton Cemetary / Daughter / of / Henry Bone R.A. / celebrated Enamel Painter.

HL to left, seated in a Regency chair and leaning forward, white silk dress, blue shawl on her right arm; brown eyes, shiny brown hair curly in front, amber ear ring, aged about 20; plain gold-brown background.
Fine rectangular gilt metal frame carved with oak leaves and acorns.

Collections: acquired from a German collection; private collection no. 63.

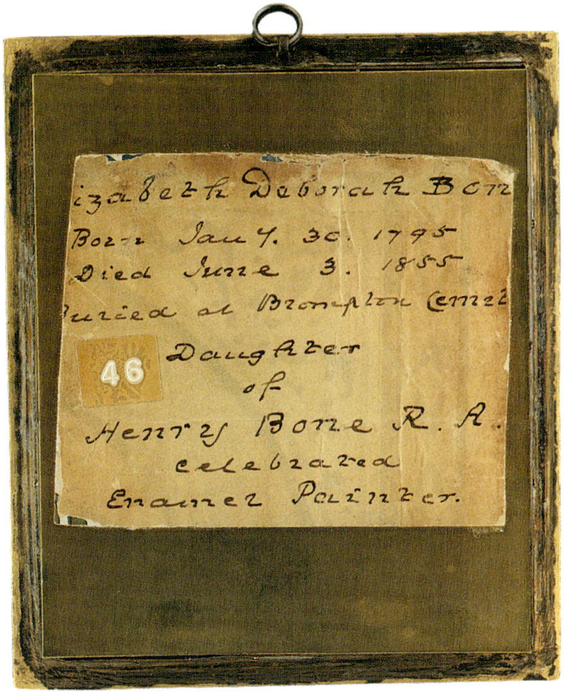
izabeth Deborah Bon
Born Jany. 30. 1795
Died June 3. 1855
uried at Brompton Cemet
46
Daughter
of
Henry Bone R.A.
celebrated
Enamel Painter.

94

Alfred Edward Chalon, 1780–1860

Princess Charlotte Augusta, c. 1817

Watercolour on card,
rectangle 104 × 84 mm (4⅛ × 3¼ in),
signed to right: *AEC* (monogram) *R.A.*

HL to right, dark red dress, green and gold shawl; brown eyes, shiny brown hair with pearl circlet, aged about 20; plain brown background. Rectangular decorated ormolu frame with clawed back.

Collections: acquired from a Hanoverian family in 1998; private collection no. 62.

Chalon was born in Geneva, brought to England aged 9, and entered the Royal Academy Schools in 1797. He exhibited miniatures in London from 1801 till he died there in 1860. He was appointed Painter in Watercolours to Queen Victoria and there are examples of his watercolours in the Royal Collection and the Victoria and Albert Museum, and of his miniatures in the National Portrait Gallery and at Powis Castle, Waddesdon Manor and Knightshayes Court. This miniature has been traditionally identified as Princess Charlotte Augusta, the Prince Regent's daughter. Chalon certainly did paint the Princess several times. As a child she had fair hair (dyed dark brown later in life) but noticeably brilliant blue eyes, and one would have expected a crown surmounting the frame.

95

John Cox Dillman Engleheart, 1784–1862

Three Sisters, 1815–25

Watercolour on ivory,
rectangle 145 × 183 mm (5¾ × 7¼ in),
uninscribed.

Three TQL figures against a red curtain and architectural background.
Rectangular gilt-wood modern frame.

Collection: private collection no. 31.

J.C.D. Engleheart was George Engleheart's nephew, pupil and assistant. His work is similar to his uncle's if sweeter and not quite so forceful, and usually painted on large rectangular ivories. The ivory often shows through the paint, as here, giving a translucence which enhances the general sugary effect. Examples of his work are in most collections, especially the Fitzwilliam Museum and Mompesson House, Salisbury.

96

John Wright, d. 1820

Henry Paget, Marquess of Anglesey, 1816

Gouache on ivory,
oval 82 × 66 mm (3¼ × 2⅝ in) sight size,
possibly signed close above the pelisse, and on the reverse signed and dated 1816.
HS facing, blue uniform of 7th Hussars, pelisse, Orders (Garter, Bath, Hanover);
brown eyes, light brown hair and whiskers, bushy eyebrows, aged 44;
sky background.
Gold locket with a single lock of dark brown hair under blue glass.

Collection: private collection no. 71.

Wright exhibited at the Royal Academy from 1795 to 1819. He committed suicide in 1820. This miniature is a copy, with variations in the Orders, of Lawrence's whole-length portrait, painted for the Marquess *c.*1816–17, and still at Plas Newydd. A similar Wright miniature, of the Duke of Northumberland 1817, is at Powis Castle (National Trust).

97

Henri Grevedon, 1776–1860

Officer in Black Uniform, 1818

Watercolour on ivory,
oval 95 × 73 mm (3¾ × 2⅞ in),
signed and dated lower right: *Henri Grevedon, 1818.*

HS to left, black uniform, gold epaulettes, high black collar and neckcloth, buttons with fleurs-de-lis, two campaign medals; hazel eyes, grey hair carefully painted and heightened with white gouache, pale face firmly modelled with blue strokes and stipple, careworn expression, aged 45–50; plain grey gouache background. Chased oval gilt-metal frame set in a plain brown wood rectangle.

Collections: de Lasalle family; private collection no. 82.

98

Henri Grevedon, 1776–1860

Officer in Scarlet Uniform, c. 1818

Watercolour on ivory,
oval 88 × 68 mm (3½ × 2⅝ in),
signed at right with flourish: *Henry Grevedon.*

HS to right, scarlet uniform with gold collar and facings, gold cords and epaulettes; brown eyes, curly black hair and whiskers, aged 20–25; plain grey background.
Framed to match No. 97.

Collections: de Lasalle family; private collection no. 83.

Henri Grevedon was born and worked in Paris. He sometimes signed his first name as 'Henry', possibly when painting portraits of British officers. The two miniatures here appear to be of French officers, possibly father and son of the de Lasalle family.

99

Nicolas François Dun, 1764–1832

Prince Achille Murat, c. 1820

Watercolour on ivory, oval 56 × 47 mm (2¼ × 1⅞ in), signed *Dun.*
HS to right in pink and gold cavalry uniform, black necktie; dark eyes, short black hair, aged about 18; plain grey background.
Plain brass frame.

Collection: private collection no. 103.

Nicolas Dun, sometimes confused with an Irish miniaturist, John Dunn, was born in France but worked mainly in Naples where he died in 1832. Prince Achille, eldest son of Napoleon's swashbuckling cavalry marshal who married Napoleon's sister, Marie-Annunziate-Carolina, and became King of Naples, was born in 1801, left Naples with his mother in 1815 for Hamburg and Vienna, and emigrated to America in 1823, where in 1826 he married Catherine Willis Gray, a great-grandniece of George Washington. He is said to have resembled Napoleon.

100

Moritz Michael Daffinger, 1790–1849

Gräfin Henrietta Hunyady, c. 1821

Watercolour on ivory,
oval 75 × 58 mm (3 × 2¼ in) sight size,
uninscribed.

HS to left, white square-cut dress, leather belt with gold buckle; grey eyes, fair curled hair with centre parting, aged about 20; foliage and sky background. Oval gilt metal case mounted on a brown velvet easel frame, all within a leather travelling case stamped *T 1872*.

Collection: private collection no. 61.

Daffinger, one of the foremost miniaturists at the Viennese Court, was born and worked in Vienna; he died in 1849. His work often shows the influence of Sir Thomas Lawrence, who was working in Vienna after Waterloo. Henrietta Hunyady, born Princess Henrietta of Lichtenstein, married Graf von Hunyady in 1821, the probable occasion of this portrait.

101

Andrew Plimer, 1763–1837

Young Lady in White, 1829

Watercolour on white paper,
rectangle 218 × 174 mm (8¼ × 6⅞ in),
signed and dated: *APlimer Pinxt 1829.*

HL to left, white dress, blue sash; blue eyes, brown curled hair with bun, right arm raised, serious expression.
Paul Mitchell rectangular gilt wood frame.

Collections: Miss Frances Dakers, a descendant of Andrew Plimer; private collection no. 81.

1829.

102

Andrew Plimer, 1763–1837

Young Lady in White, c. 1829

Watercolour on white paper,
octagonal 199 × 168 mm (7⅞ × 6⅝ in),
uninscribed.

TQL seated facing, head to left, white dress with puffed sleeves and white waist band; blue eyes, short dark hair with centre parting, aged 25–30; sky background. Framed to match No. 101.

Literature: Williamson 1903, pp. 64–5.
Collections: as for No. 101; private collection no. 80.

For Plimer's earlier work see Nos. 59 and 60. By 1829 he was 66 and had given up miniature painting in favour of large coloured drawings on paper – less expensive than ivory and also less exacting on the eyes. These two drawings are typical examples. In 1801 he married Joanna Knight, a sister of his pupil, Mary Ann Knight. They had five children, Louisa, Charlotte, Selina, Joanna and Andrew. The two young women here are probably Charlotte and Selina.

103

Edward Robert Hughes, 1851–1914

William Holman Hunt, O.M., c. 1880

Watercolour on ivory,
oval 42 × 34 mm (1 5/8 × 1 3/8 in),
uninscribed.

HS facing; luxuriant red beard, blue eyes, pale face, aged 53; green background. Silver filigree frame set with 'jewels' and engraved: *W. Holman Hunt O.M. / Aetat 53.*

Collections: bought from a descendant of Holman Hunt's housekeeper; private collection no. 74.

Hughes was a fellow student with Holman Hunt at the Royal Academy Schools, became a close friend and often worked as his assistant. The miniature is a copy of Holman Hunt's threequarter-length self-portrait, painted in 1880 for the Uffizi Gallery, Florence. Another full-sized copy, painted possibly by Hughes also and used for this miniature copy, is in the Athenaeum Club, London, presented by Mrs Holman Hunt. William Holman Hunt, one of the founders of the Pre-Raphaelite Brotherhood, painted many famous pictures, such as *The Hireling Shepherd*, *The Light of the World* and *The Scapegoat.*

Bibliography

BAYNE-POWELL 1985. Robert Bayne-Powell, *Catalogue of Portrait Miniatures in the Fitzwilliam Museum*, 1985

BAYNE-POWELL 1992. Robert Bayne-Powell, *Catalogue of Miniatures in the Holburne Museum*, 1992

CONNOR 1993. P. Connor, *George Chinnery*, 1993

COOMBS 1998. Katherine Coombs, *The Portrait Miniature in England*, 1998

DEJARDIN 1997. Ian Dejardin, Sebastian Edwards and Aileen Ribeiro, *Miniatures at Kenwood: the Draper Gift*, 1997

FINSTON 1981. Jill Finston, *Isaac Oliver*, 2 vols., 1981

FOSKETT 1964. Daphne Foskett, *John Smart: the Man and his Miniatures*, 1964

FREDEMAN 1965. William Fredeman, *Pre-Raphaelites*, 1965

HUNT 1969. Diana Holman Hunt, *My Grandfather, His Wives and Loves*, 1969

LAVENDER 1993. D. S. Lavender, *The Monarchy in Portrait Miniatures from Elizabeth I to Queen Victoria*, 1993 (exhibition catalogue)

LLOYD 1995. Stephen Lloyd, *Richard and Maria Cosway*, 1995 (exhibition catalogue)

LLOYD 1999. Stephen Lloyd, *Raeburn's Rival, Archibald Skirving, 1749–1819*, 1999

MURDOCH 1997. John Murdoch, *Seventeenth-century English Miniatures*, 1997

MURDOCH 1988. John Murdoch, Jim Murrell, Patrick J. Noon, and Roy Strong, *The English Miniature*, 1988

REYNOLDS 1988. Graham Reynolds, *English Portrait Miniatures*, 1952, revised 1988

STRONG 1969. Roy Strong, *Tudor and Jacobean Portraits*, 1969

STRONG 1984. Roy Strong, *The English Renaissance Miniature*, 1983, revised 1984

SUMNER 1996. Ann Sumner (ed.), *Death, Passion and Politics*, 1996 (exhibition catalogue)

SUMNER 1998. Ann Sumner, *The Collector's Eye*, 1998 (exhibition catalogue)

WALKER 1992. Richard Walker, *Miniatures in the Collection of Her Majesty the Queen*, 1992

WILLIAMSON 1902. G.C. Williamson and Henry Engleheart, *George Engleheart 1750–1829, Miniature Painter to George III*, 1902; contains Engleheart's Fee Book

WILLIAMSON 1903. G.C. Williamson, *Andrew and Nathaniel Plimer*, 1903

WILLIAMSON 1906. G.C. Williamson, *Catalogue of the Collection of Miniatures, the property of J. Pierpont Morgan*, 4 vols., 1906–8; sold at Christie's 24–7 June 1935

Wood Memorandum 1789–1809. William Wood, *Memorandum of Miniatures*, MSS in Victoria and Albert Museum Library

Index of Artists

Numerals refer to the Catalogue numbers

Barry, John (*fl.* 1784–1827) *21*
Beechey, Sir William (after) *70*
Bogle, John (1746–1803) *56*
British School (17th century) *4*
British School (18th century) *20*
Burch, Henry Jacob (1763–after 1834) *65*

Chalon, Alfred Edward (1780–1860) *93–4*
Chinnery, George (1774–1852) *92*
Collas, Louis-Antoine (*c.* 1775–after 1833) *89*
Collins, Richard (1755–1831) *84*
Cooper, Alexander (?1609–*c.* 1660) *5*
Cosway, Richard (1742–1821) *27–35*
Cross, Peter (*c.* 1645–1724) *12*
Crosse, Richard (1742–1810) *64*

Daffinger, Moritz Michael (1790–1849) *100*
Daniel, Abraham (d. 1806) *36–8*
Daniel, Joseph (*c.* 1760–1803) *39*
Day, Thomas (*c.* 1732–1807) *41*
Des Granges, David (*c.* 1611–71/2) *11*
Devis, Arthur (*c.* 1711–87) *16*
Dun, Nicolas-François (1764–1832) *99*

Edridge, Henry (1768–1821) *68–9*
Engleheart, George (1750–1829) *45–54, 75–9*
Engleheart, John Cox Dillman (1784–1862) *95*

Ferrière, François (1752–1839) *67*
Finucane, Mathias (*fl. c.* 1798) *71*
Freese, N. (*fl.* 1794–1814) *91*
French School (17th century) *8*
French School (18th century) *19*

Grevedon, Henri (1776–1860) *97–8*

Hargreaves, Thomas (1774–1846/7) *85–8*
Hilliard, Nicholas (1547–1619) *1*
Hone, Horace (1754–1825) *57–8*
Hughes, Edward Robert (1851–1914) *103*

Isabey, Jean-Baptiste (1767–1855) *90*

Jean, Philip (1755–1802) *42–4*
Johnson, Cornelius (1593–1661) *6–7*

Kean, Michael (1761–1823) *61*
Kügelgen, Franz Gerhard von (1772–1820) *82–3*

Lens, Bernard (1682–1740) *15*

Massé, Jean-Baptiste (1687–1767) *18*
Meyer, Jeremiah (1735–89) *22*

Nattier, Jean-Marc (1685–1766) *17*
Netscher, Caspar (1635/6–84) *10*

Oliver, Isaac (*c.*1565–1617) *2–3*

Plimer, Andrew (1763–1837) *59–60, 101–2*

Richter, Christian (1678–1732) *12*
Rigaud, Hyacinthe (1659–1743) *14*
Rouvier, Pierre (*fl.* 1770–1800) *63*

Shirreff, Charles (*c.*1750–*c.*1831) *66*
Sicardi, Louis-Marie (1746–1825) *62*
Skirving, Archibald (1749–1819) *72*
Smart, John (1742/3–1811) *23–6, 80–1*
Smiadecki, Franciszek (late 17th century) *9*

'V' (*fl. c.* 1775–80) *40*
Voille, Jean-Louis (1744–*c.* 1802) *55*

White, Robert (1645–1703) *13*
Wood, William (1769–1810) *73–4*
Wright, John (d. 1820) *96*

Index of Portraits

Numerals refer to the Catalogue numbers

Alexander I, Tsar *55*
Alexandra, daughter of Tsar Paul I *55*
Alington, Lord *9*
Alison, Revd Archibald *41*
Amelia, Princess *70*
Anglesey, Henry Paget, Marquess of *96*
Augustus, Duke of Sussex *35*

Bingham, Lady Elizabeth *34*
Bone, Elizabeth *93*

Catherine, daughter of Tsar Paul I *55*
Champneys, General *84*
Channing, Miss *54*
Charles II *11*
Charlotte Augusta, Princess *38, 94*
Constantine, son of Tsar Paul I *55*

d'Orléans, Gaston *5*

Essex, Robert Devereux, 2nd Earl of *2*

Fitzherbert, Mrs *31*
Flint, Sir Charles and Lady *78–9*

Gale, Major Henry Richmond *32*

Greer, Marian *92*

Helena, daughter of Tsar Paul I *55*
Hunt, William Holman *103*
Hunyady, Henrietta, Countess *100*

Inglis, Catherine *52*

Leicester, Dorothy, Countess of *3*
Leigh family *85–7*

Mackintosh, Lieutenant John *33*
Maria Feodorovna, Empress *55*, *82*
Marie, daughter of Tsar Paul I *55*
Mountjoy, Luke Gardiner, Viscount *51*
Murat, Achille, Prince *99*

Napoleon *90*

O'Connor, Major *20*

Pauline, Queen of Württemberg *89*
Peterborough, Carey, Countess of *12*
Phillipson, Mrs *30*
Plimer daughters *101–2*
Pompadour, Madame de *17*
Prescott, General Robert *56*

Robinson, 'Perdita' *29*
Rush, Sir William and Lady Beaumarris *73–4*

St Leger, Colonel John Hayes *61*
Sawbridge, Anne *28*
Sealy, Marmaduke *69*
Stephens, Mrs Samuel *53*
Sussex, Augustus, Duke of *35*

Tennant, John *16*
Thurn und Taxis, Theresa von *83*

Unknown Man, 16th century *1*
Unknown Men, 17th century *4*, *6–8*, *13*
Unknown Men, 18th century *19*, *22*, *25–6*, *39–40*, *43–4*, *57–8*, *64*, *67–8*, *71–2*, *76*
Unknown Men, 19th century *87*, *97–8*
Unknown Woman, 17th century *10*
Unknown Women, 18th century *14*, *23–4*, *27*, *37*, *42*, *45*, *47–50*, *59–60*, *62–3*, *65*, *75*, *77*
Unknown Women, 19th century *85–6*, *88*, *91*, *95*, *101–2*
Unknown Children *18*, *36*, *38*, *46*

White, Miss Lydia *66*
Williams, Admiral and Mrs Robert *80–81*
Wootton, John *15*
Württemberg, Pauline, Queen of *89*
Wyndham, William *21*